AF599257

THE FUNKY FISH BOOK

BY

KENNON JAMES

FOR TANIS AND ZAK

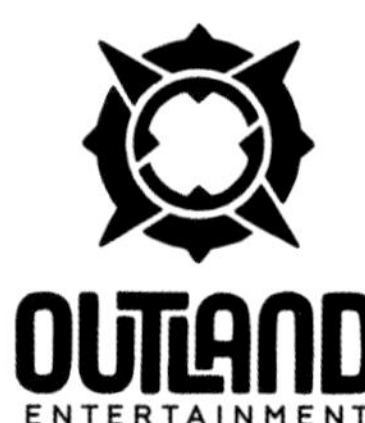

HARDCOVER ISBN: 978-1-954255-56-2

Publisher & Creative Director
Jeremy D. Mohler
Editor in Chief
Alana Joli Abbot

3119 Gillham Road
Kansas City MO, 64109
P. 785.640.4324
Email. jeremy@outlandentertainment.com

WWW.OUTLANDENTERTAINMENT.COM

THE FUNKY FISH BOOK
First Printing. Published by Outland Entertainment LLC, 3119 Gillham Road, Kansas City MO, 64109.

For international rights, please contact: jeremy@outlandentertainment.com.

Created in the United States of America.
Printed and bound in China.

WHY FISH?

I'VE GOTTEN THAT QUESTION A LOT.
IT'S AS SIMPLE AS JUST WANTING TO DRAW FISH. A FEW YEARS AGO I REALIZED I WASN'T VERY GOOD AT DRAWING FISH AND DECIDED TO PRACTICE. IT TURNED INTO A SOMEWHAT DAILY EXERCISE. THESE DRAWINGS ARE THE RESULT.

I HOPE YOU LIKE THEM.

-KENNON
APRIL 2008

SABERTOOTH ALLEY CATFISH

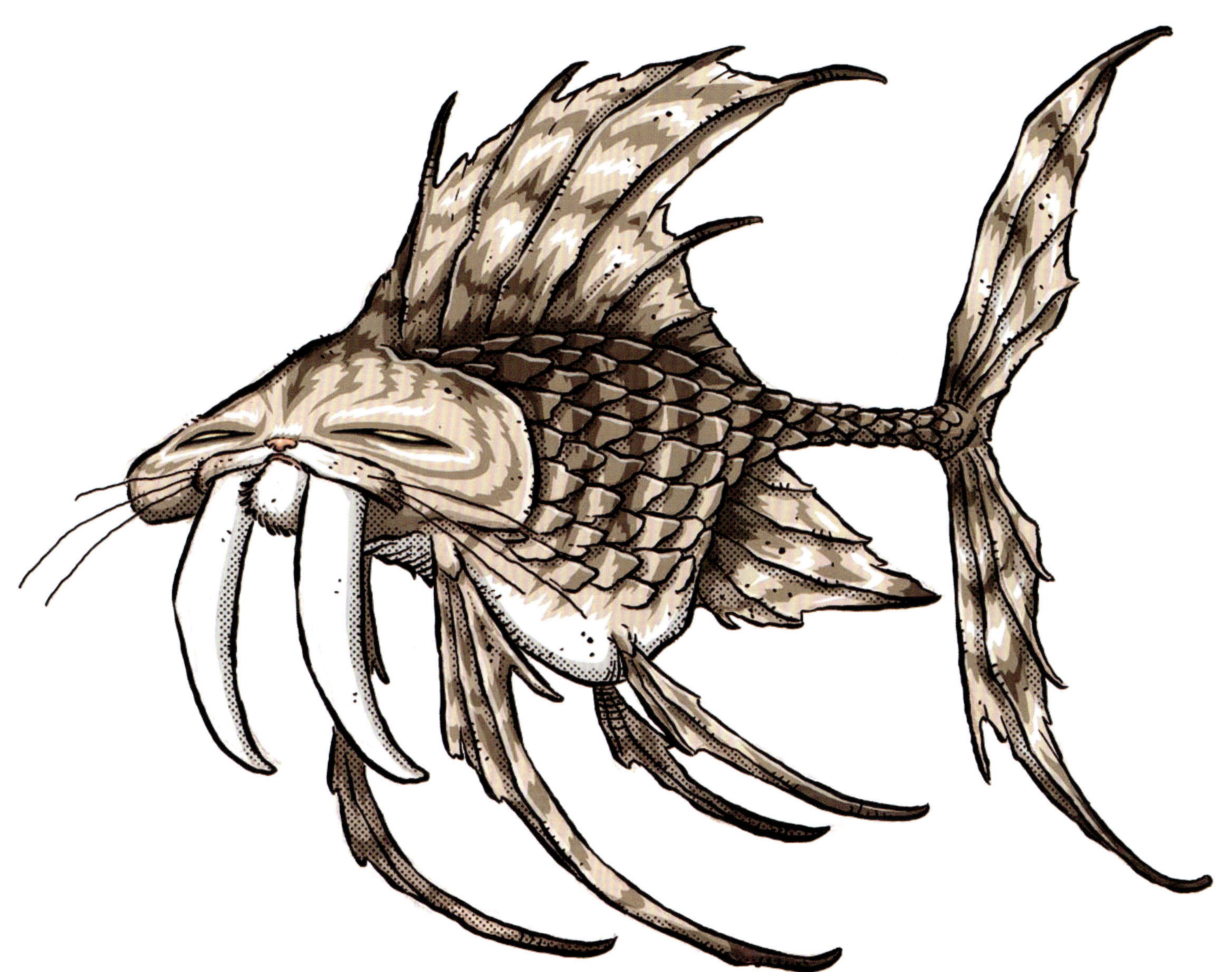

VILLAIN FISH

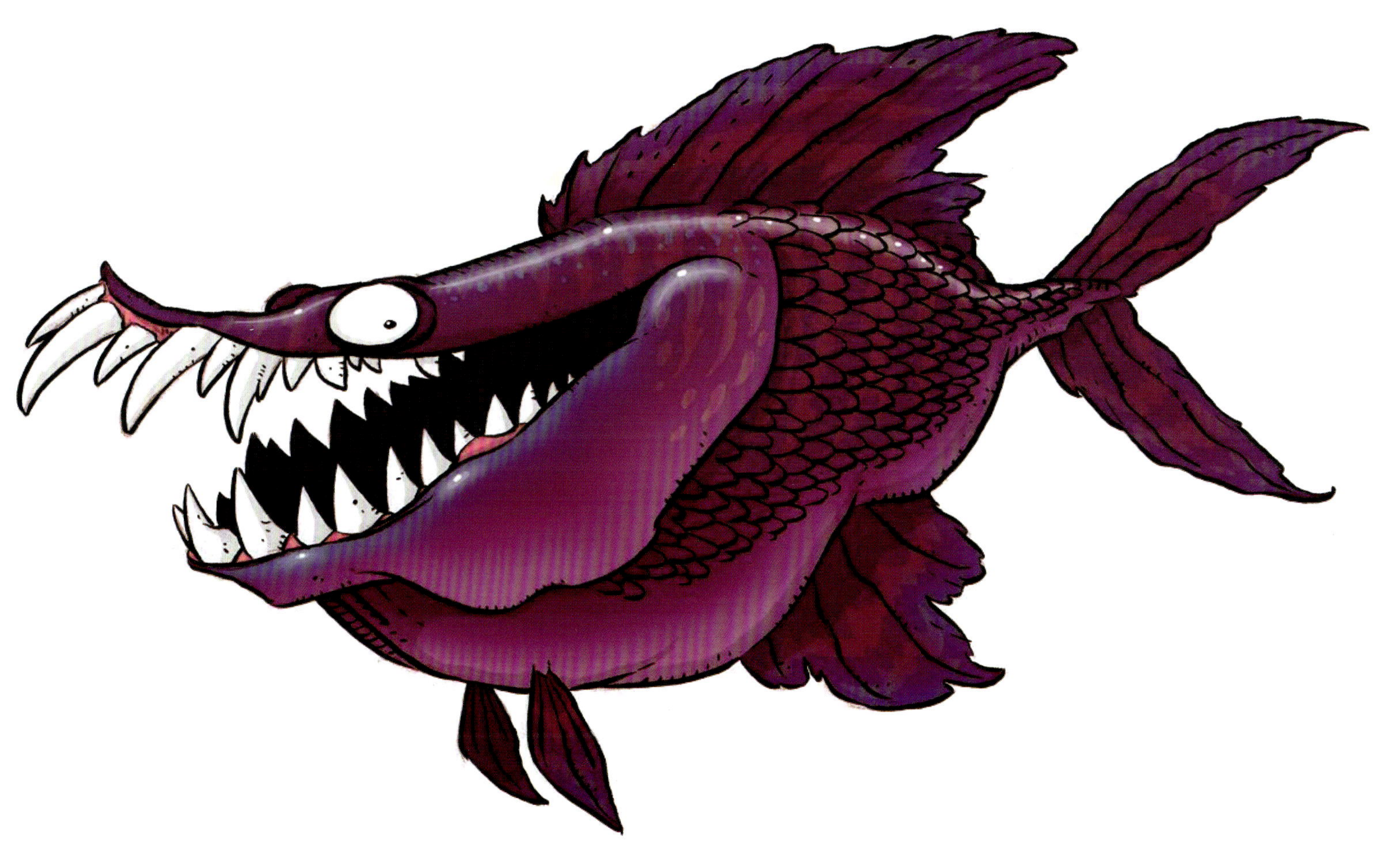

BOTTOM-DWELLING SCALLOP LICKER

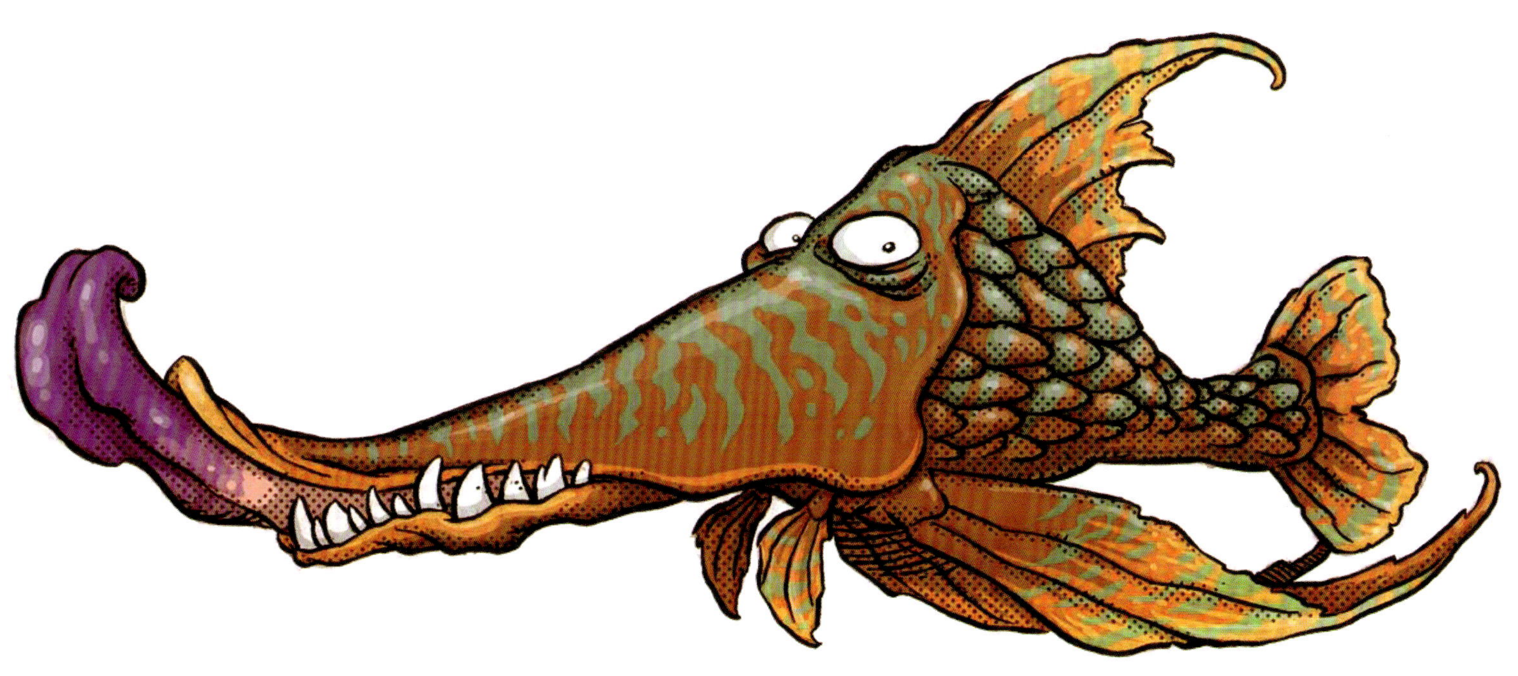

WOOLLY MAMMOTH GOLDFISH

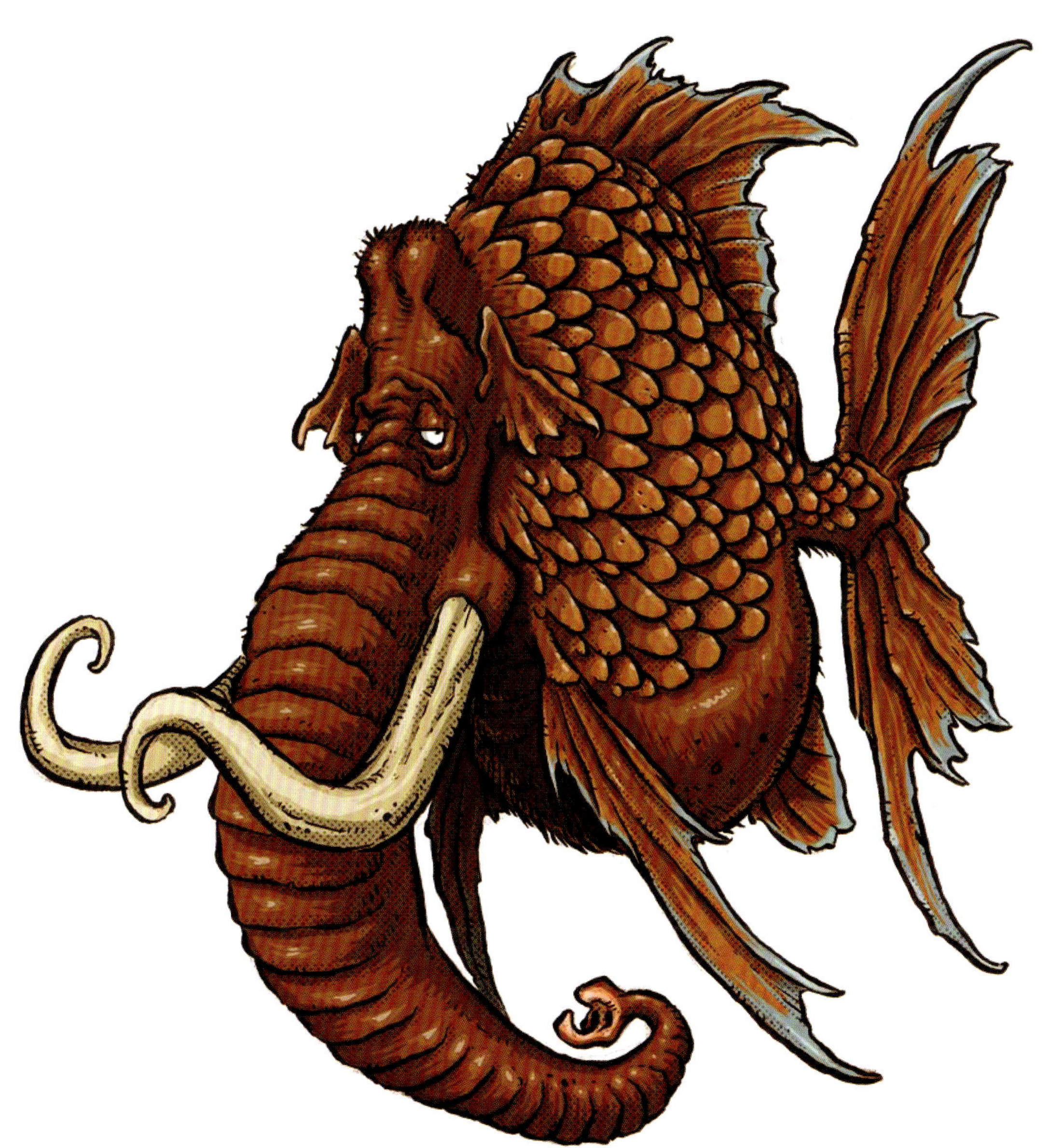

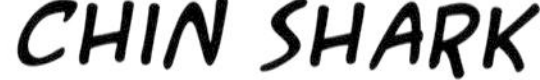
CHIN SHARK

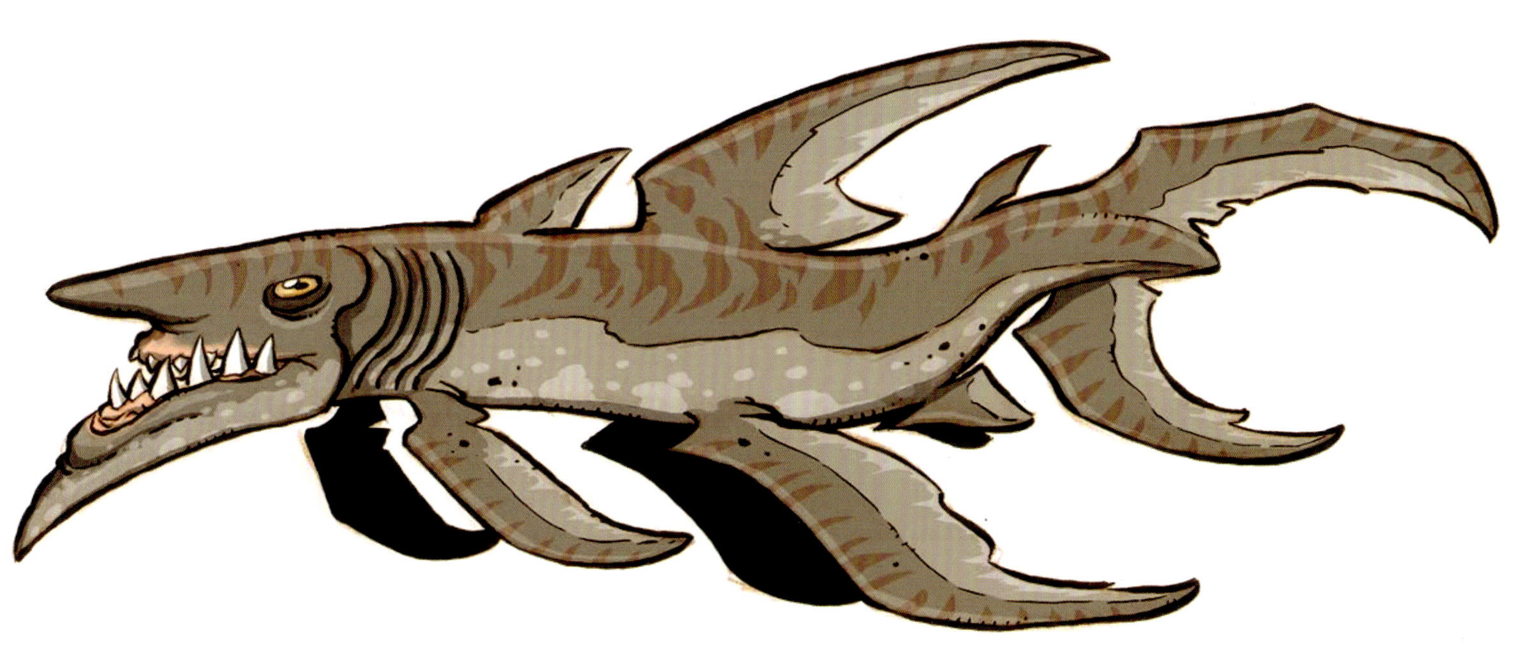

SABERTOOTH TABBY CATFISH

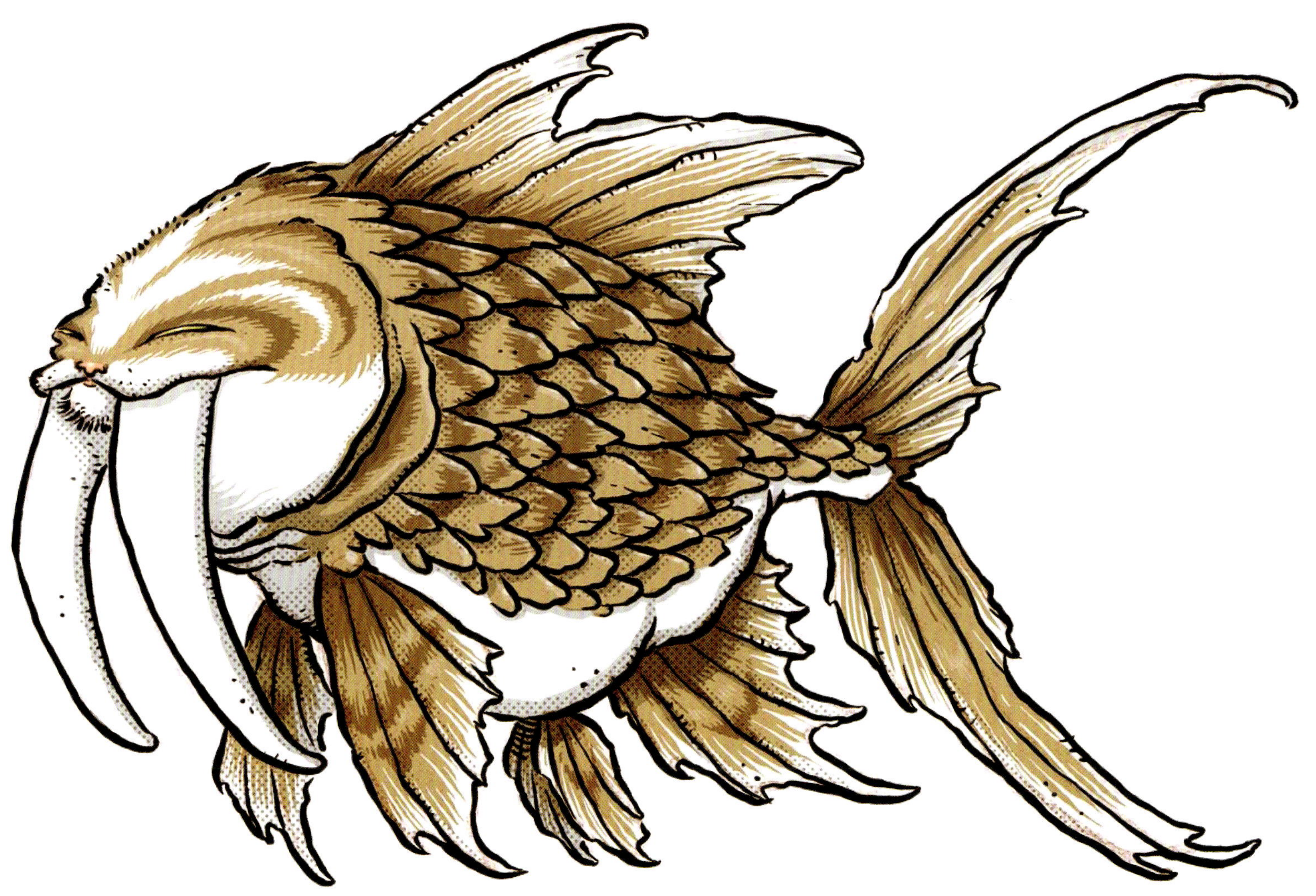

BUCKTOOTH WHISKERSNOUT

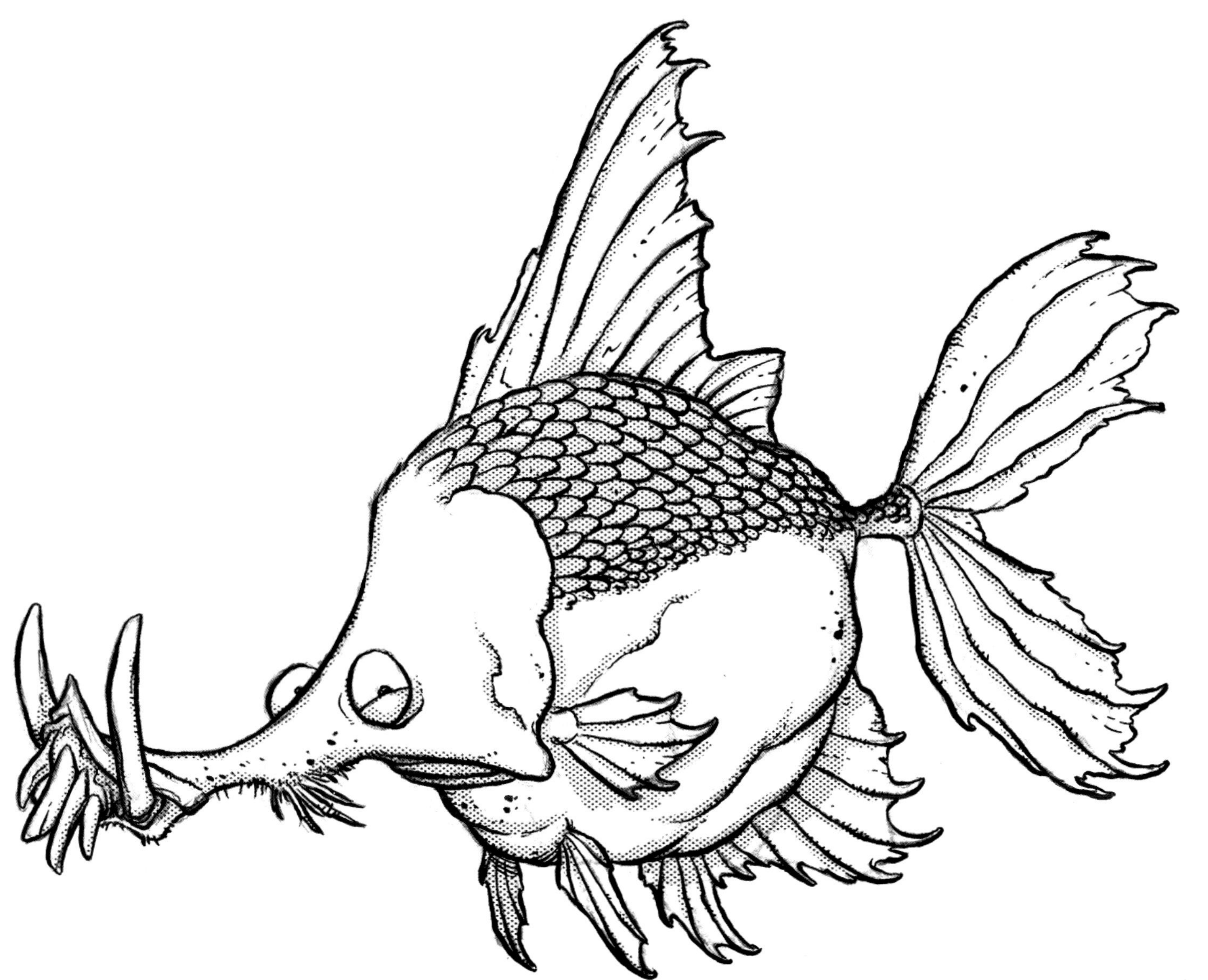

BIGFIN WEASELFISH

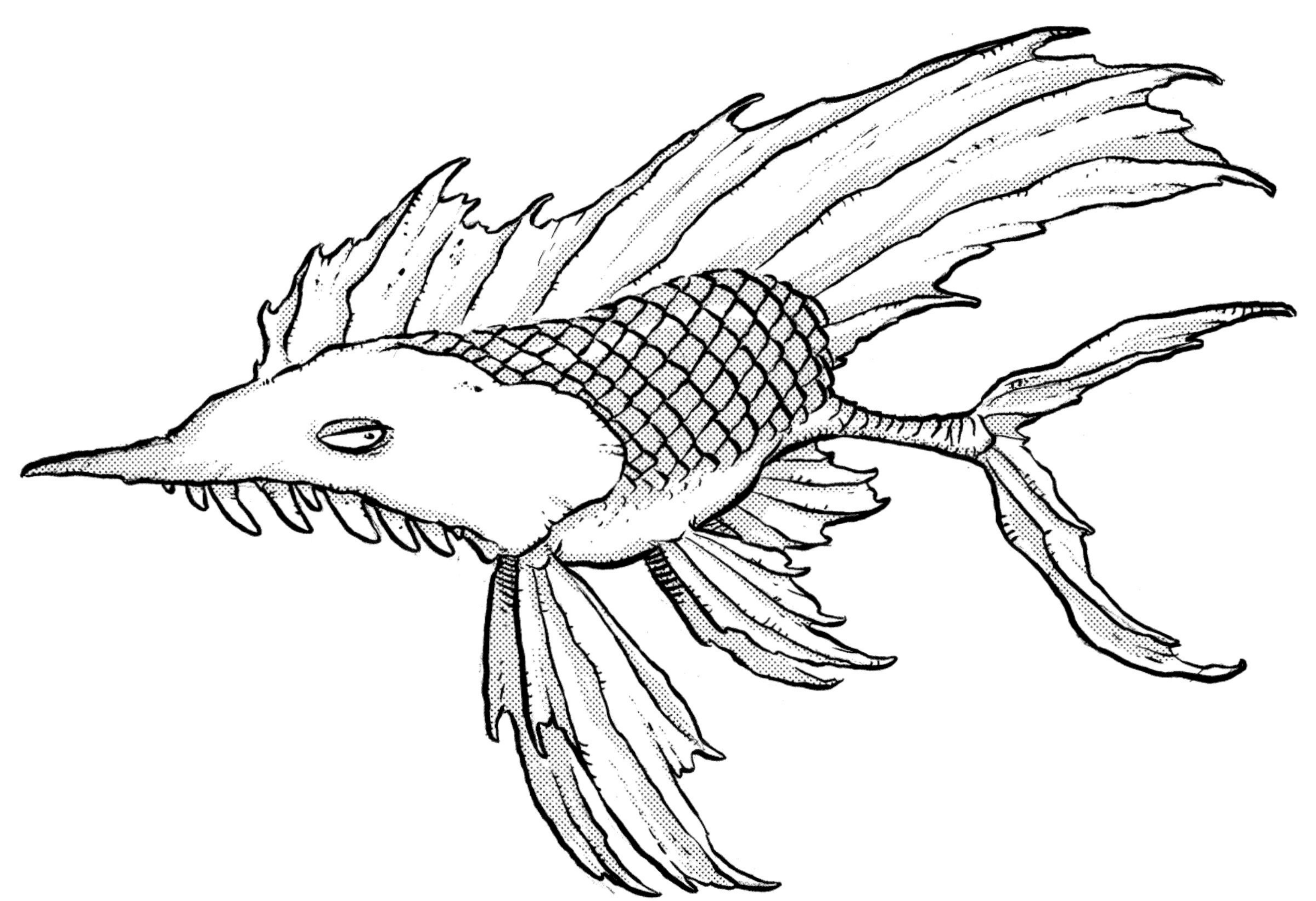

BIGHORN TROLLFISH

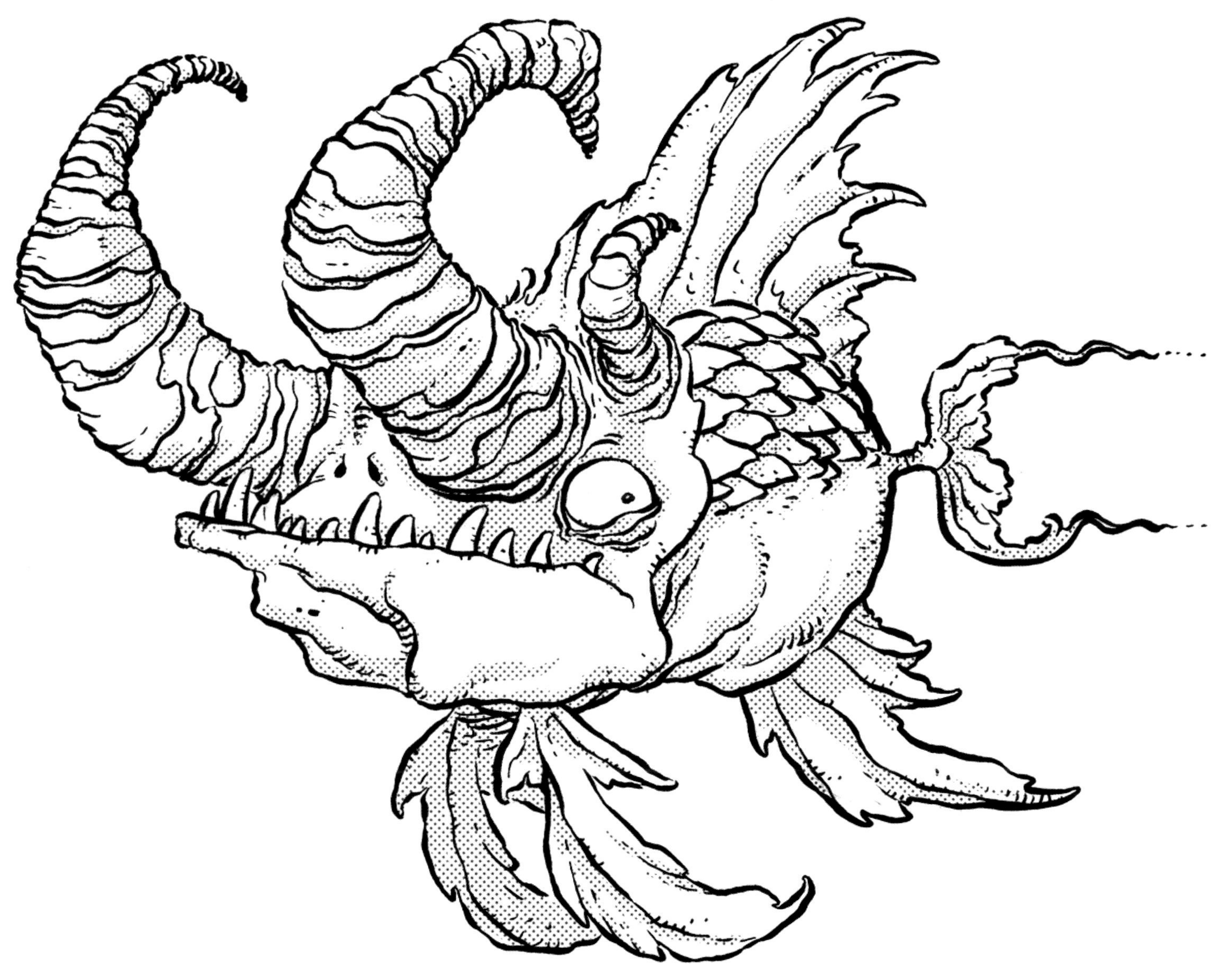

STRIPED BEAKSNOUT

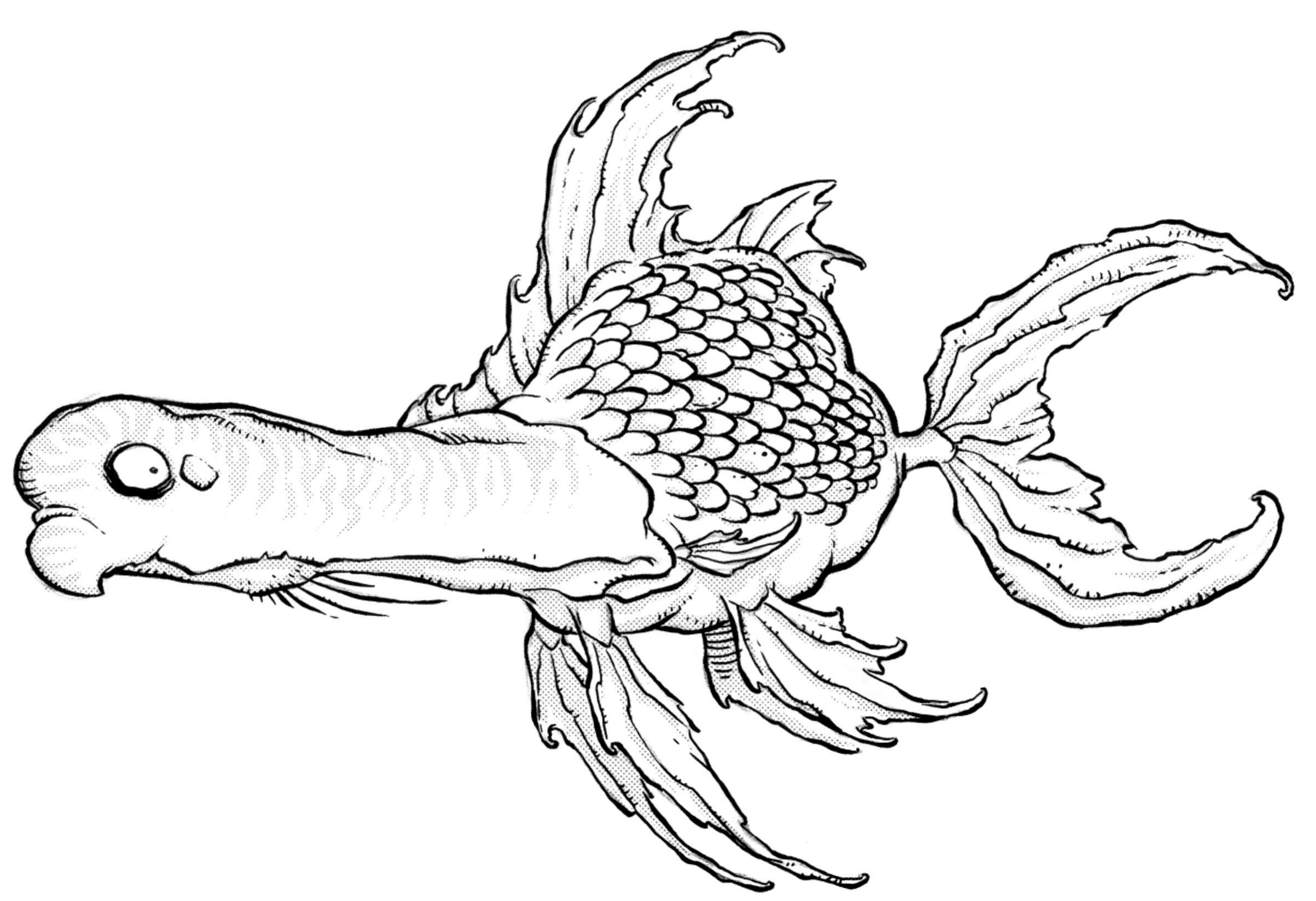

ARMORED GULLET FISH

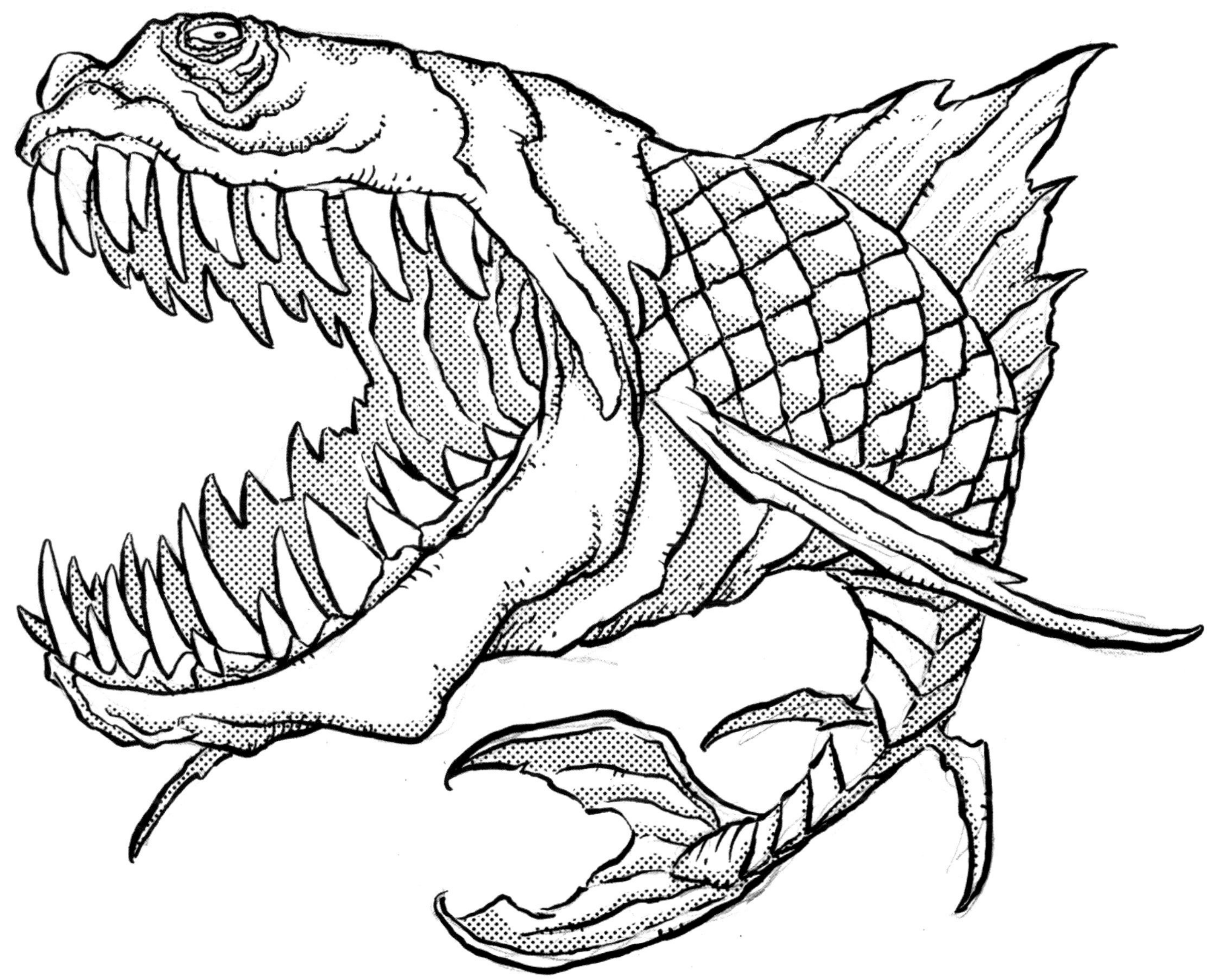

UNICORN FISH

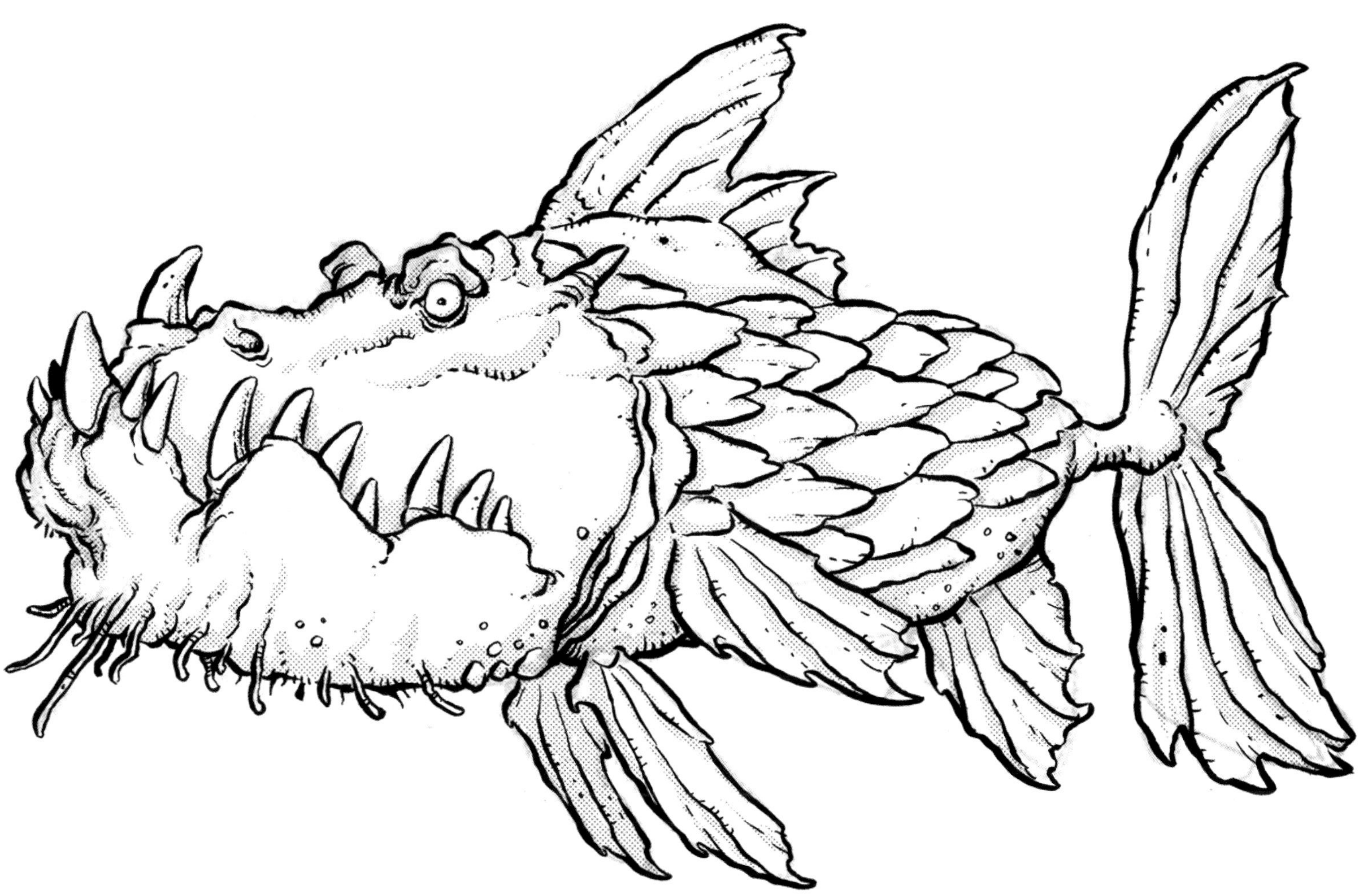

DRAGON MOOR

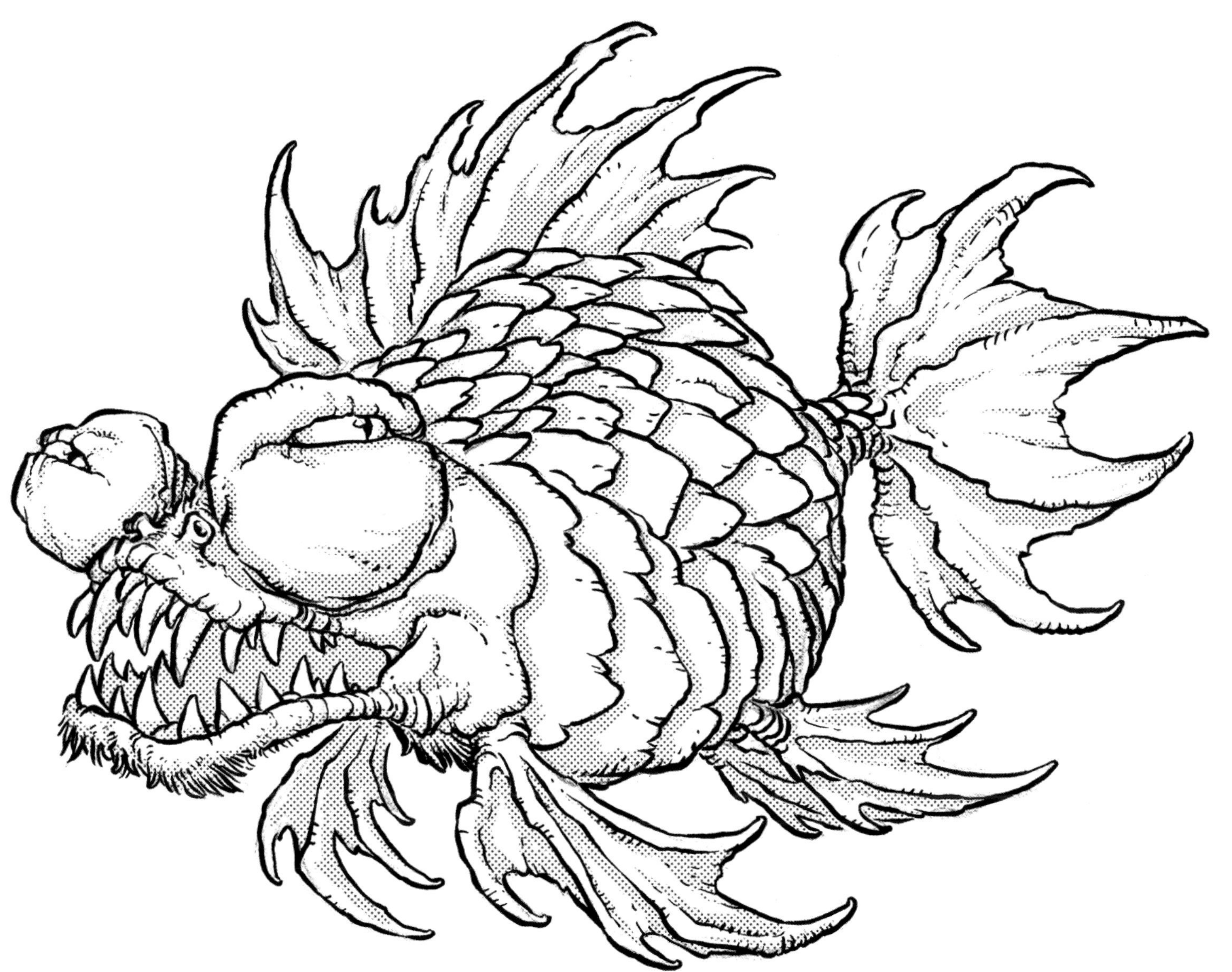

BEARDED TRIGGERFISH

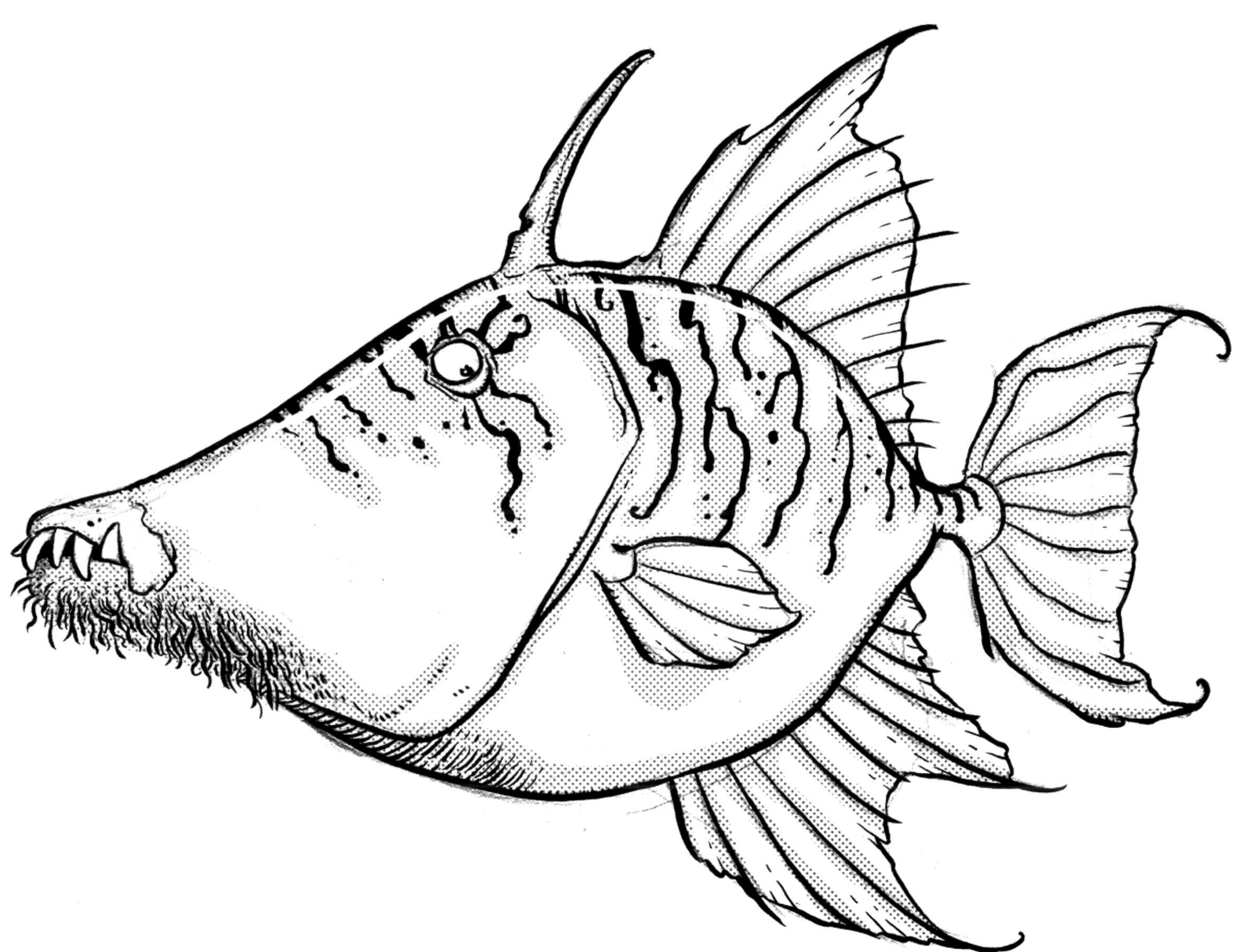

IRRITABLE CHIN FISH

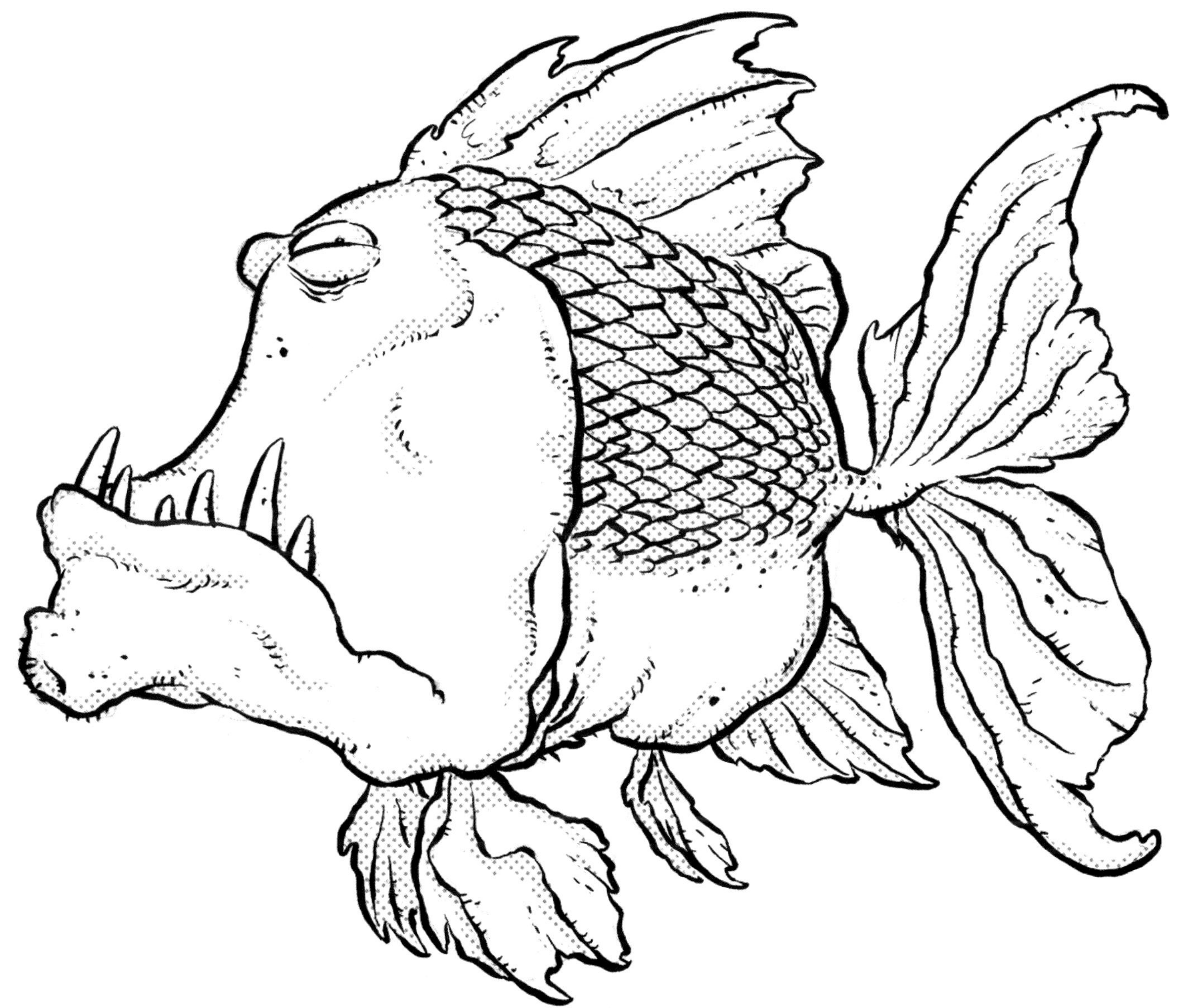

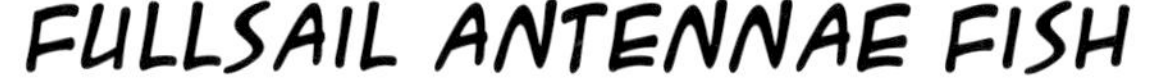
FULLSAIL ANTENNAE FISH

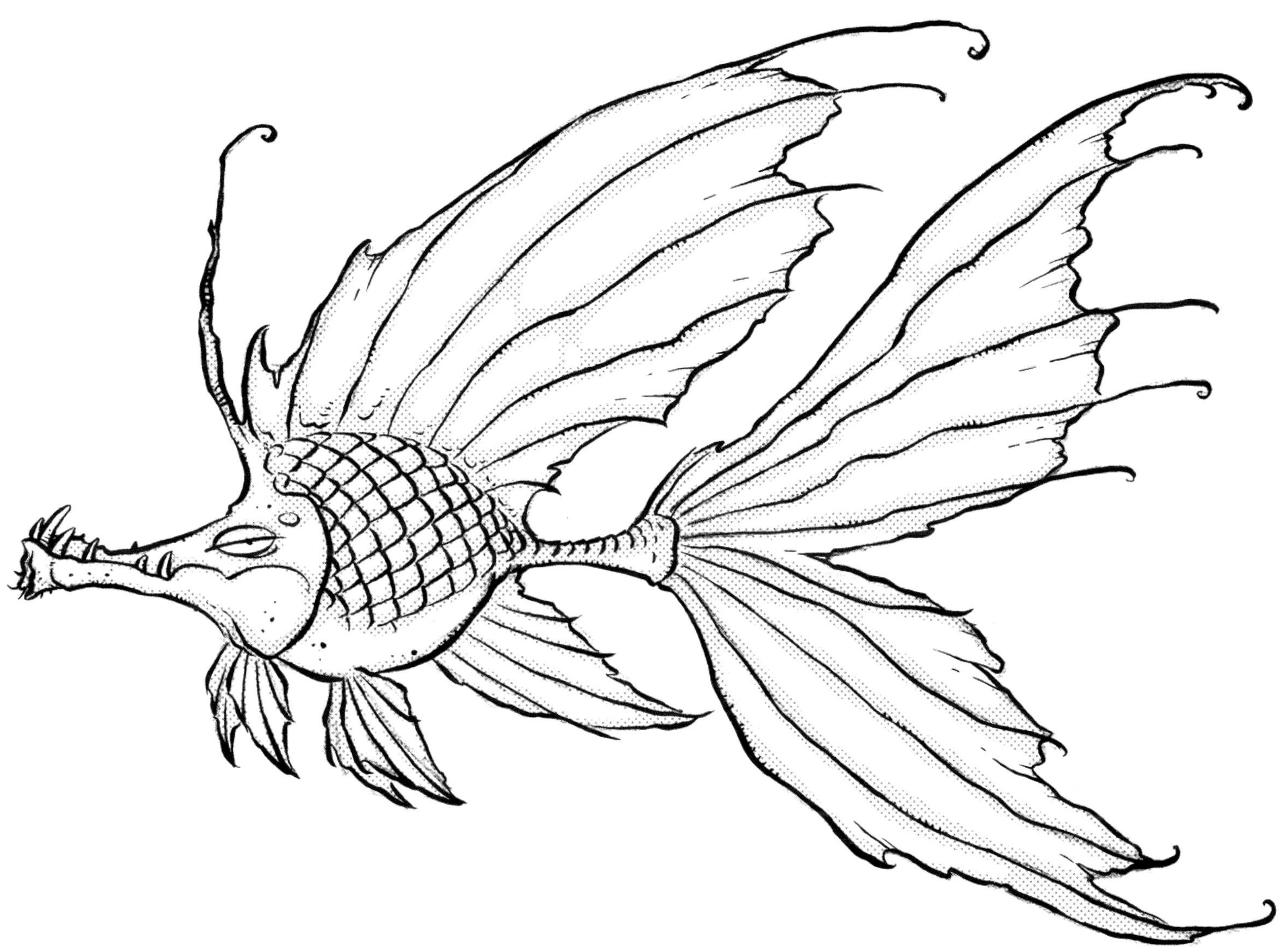

GOOFY LONGSNOUT

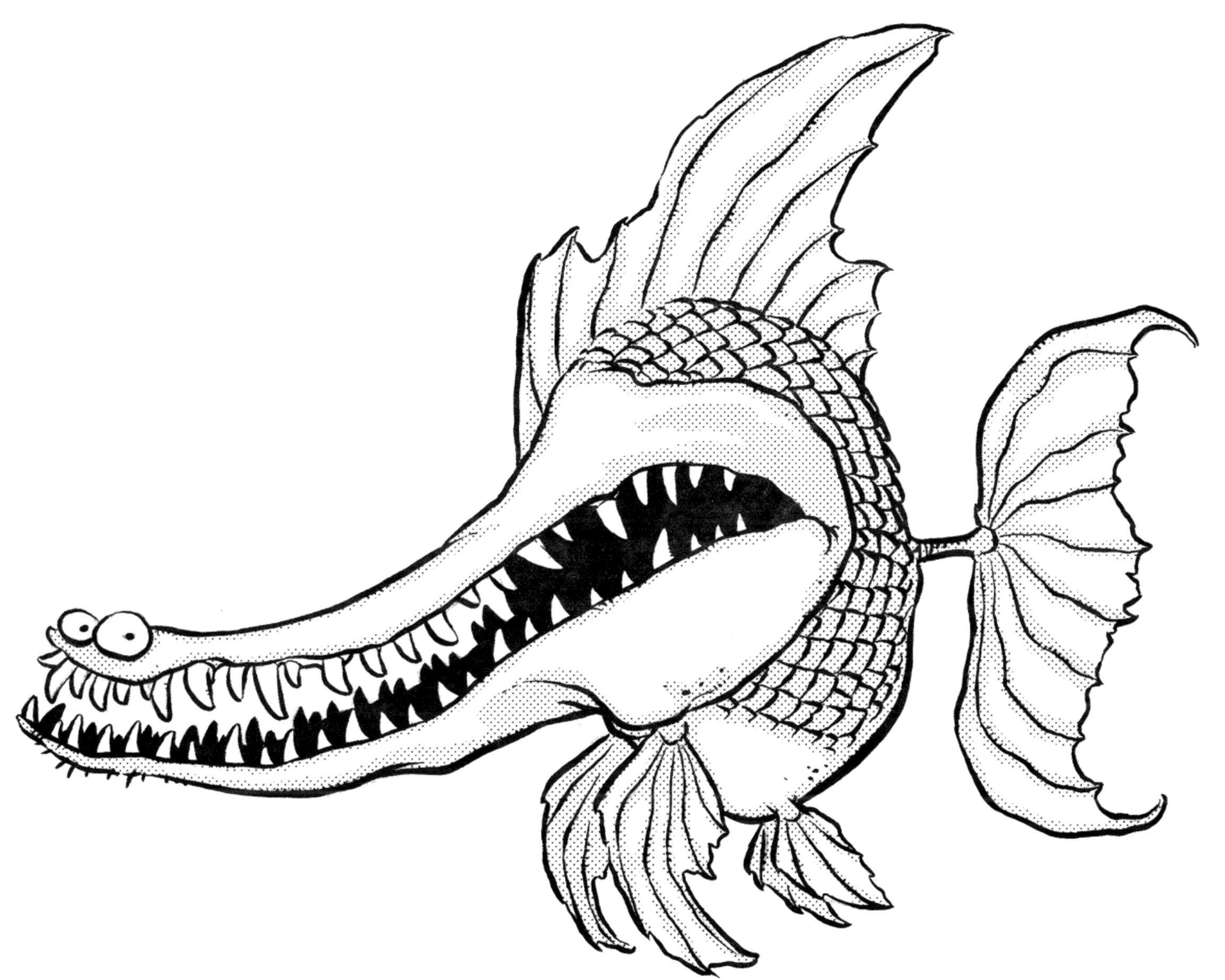

LANQUID BENTSNOUT

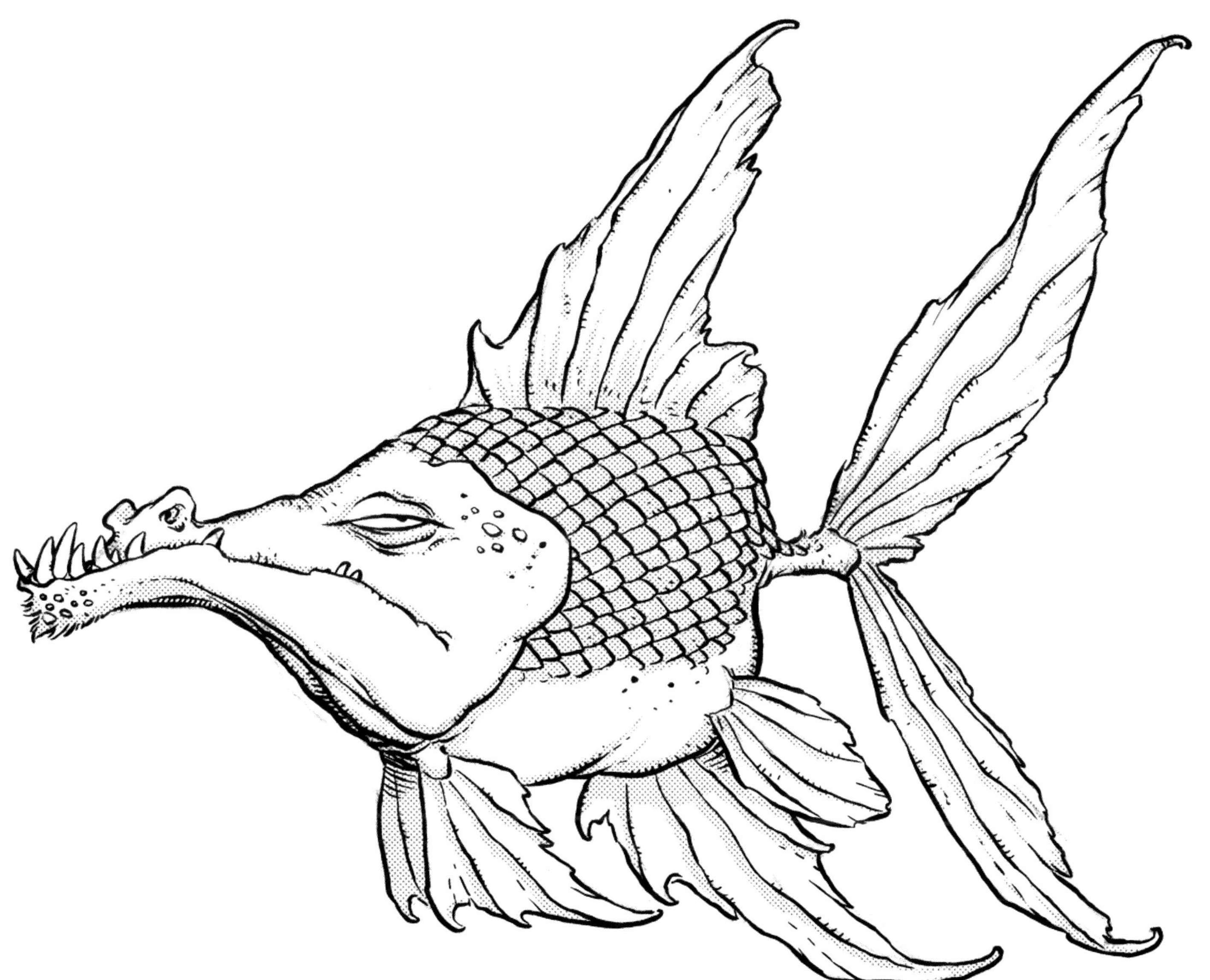

SCALY PICKJAW

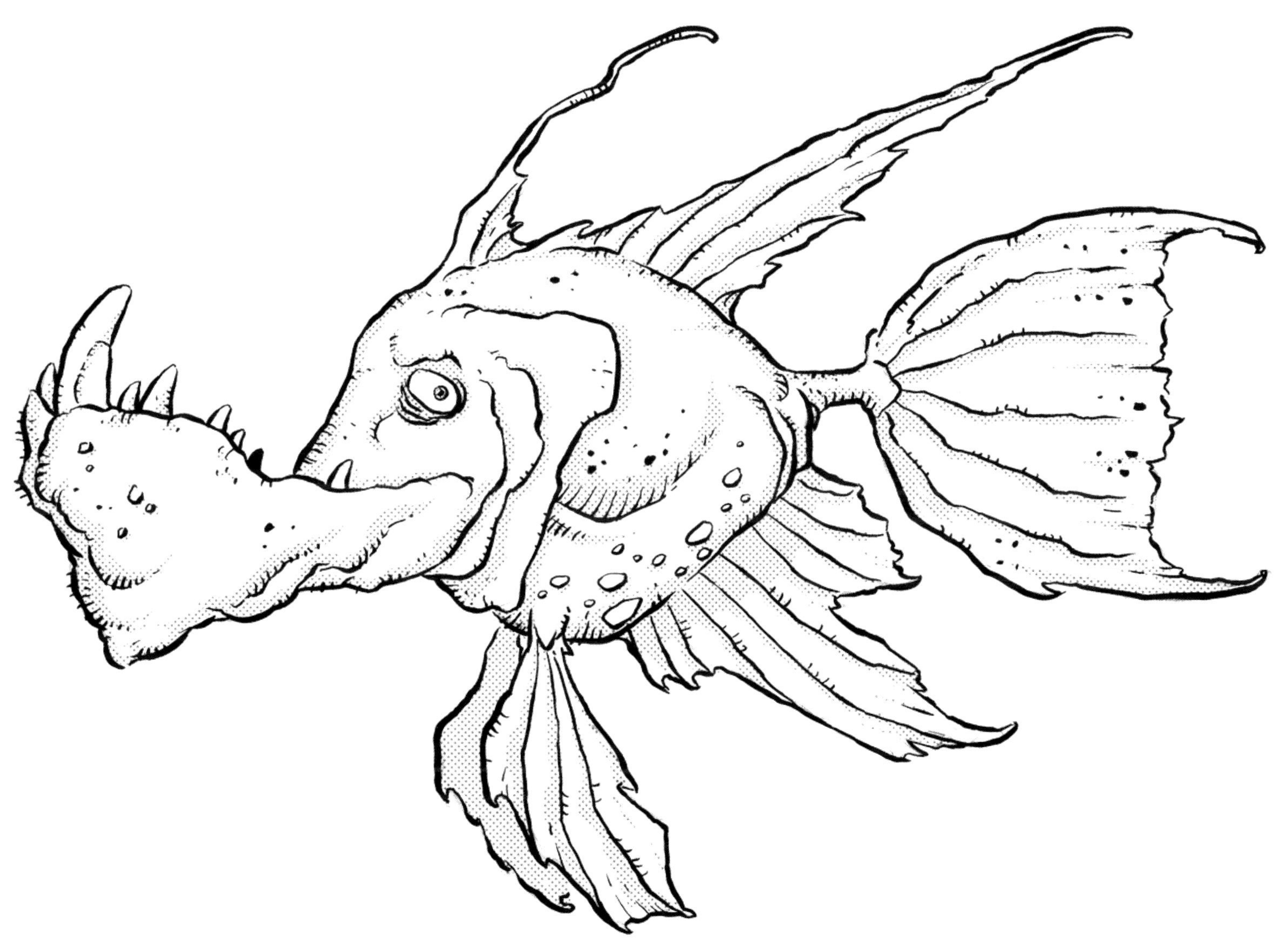

PARANOID PERCH

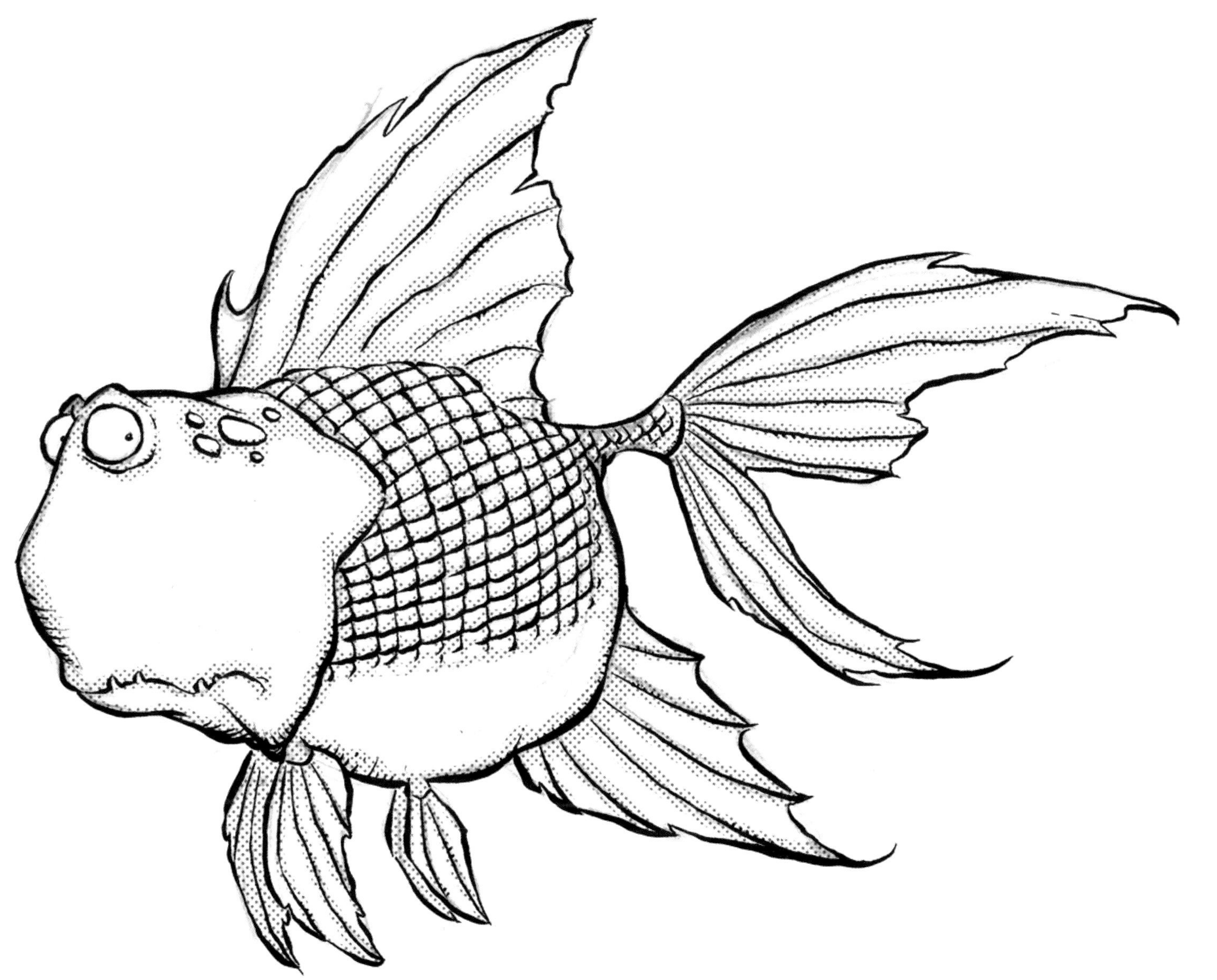

SQUINTEYE HEAVYJAW

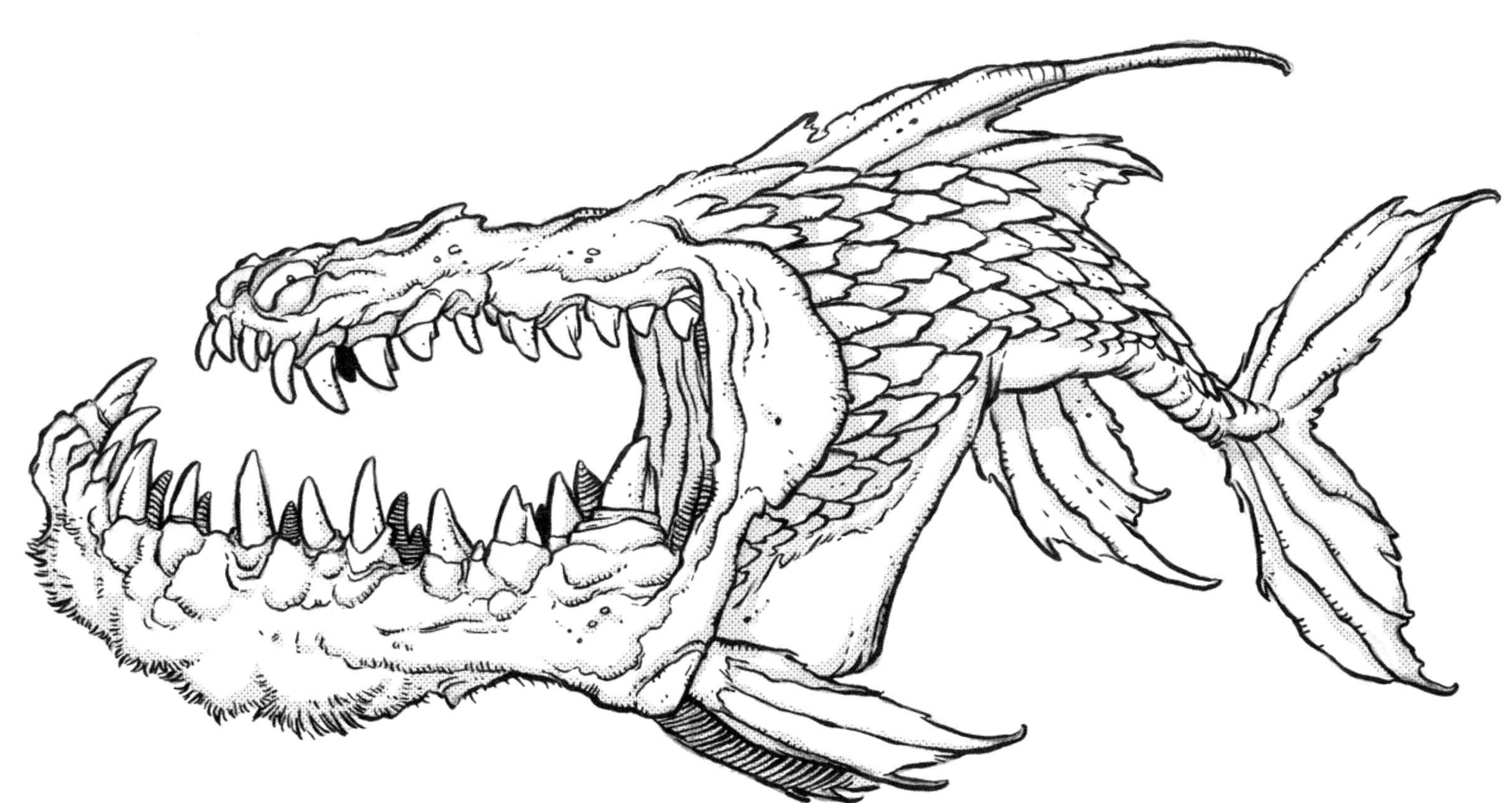

LONG-SCALED MOUSTACHE FISH

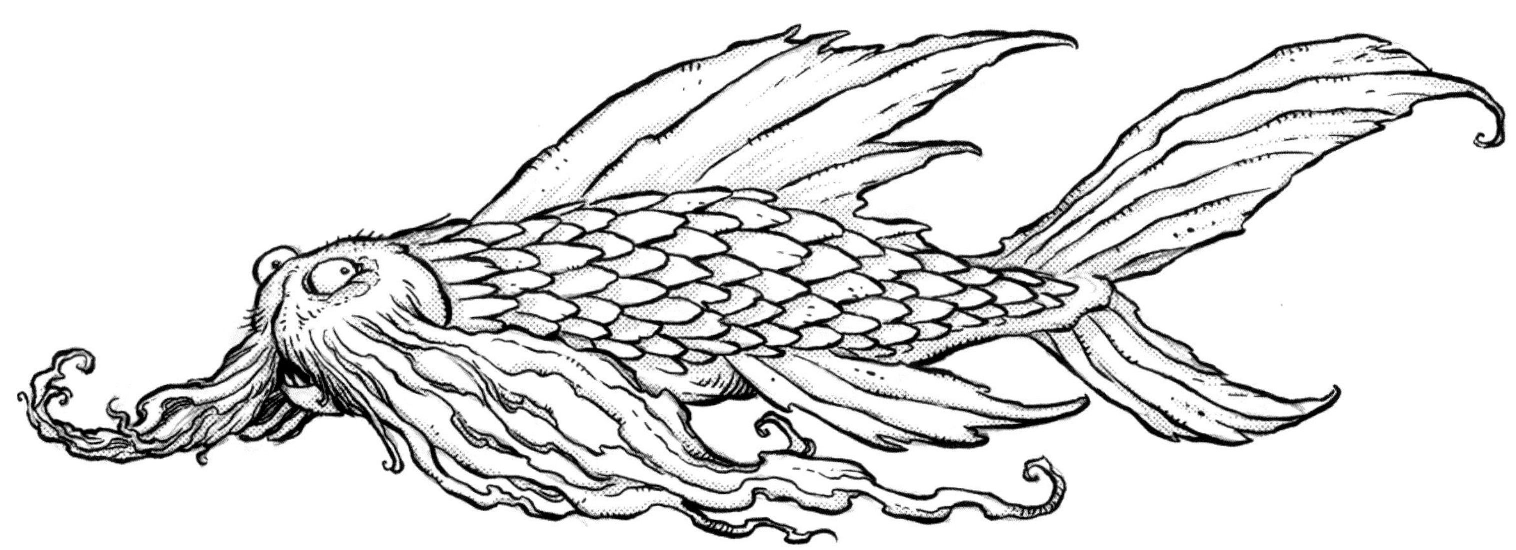

GNARLED DRAGONHEAD

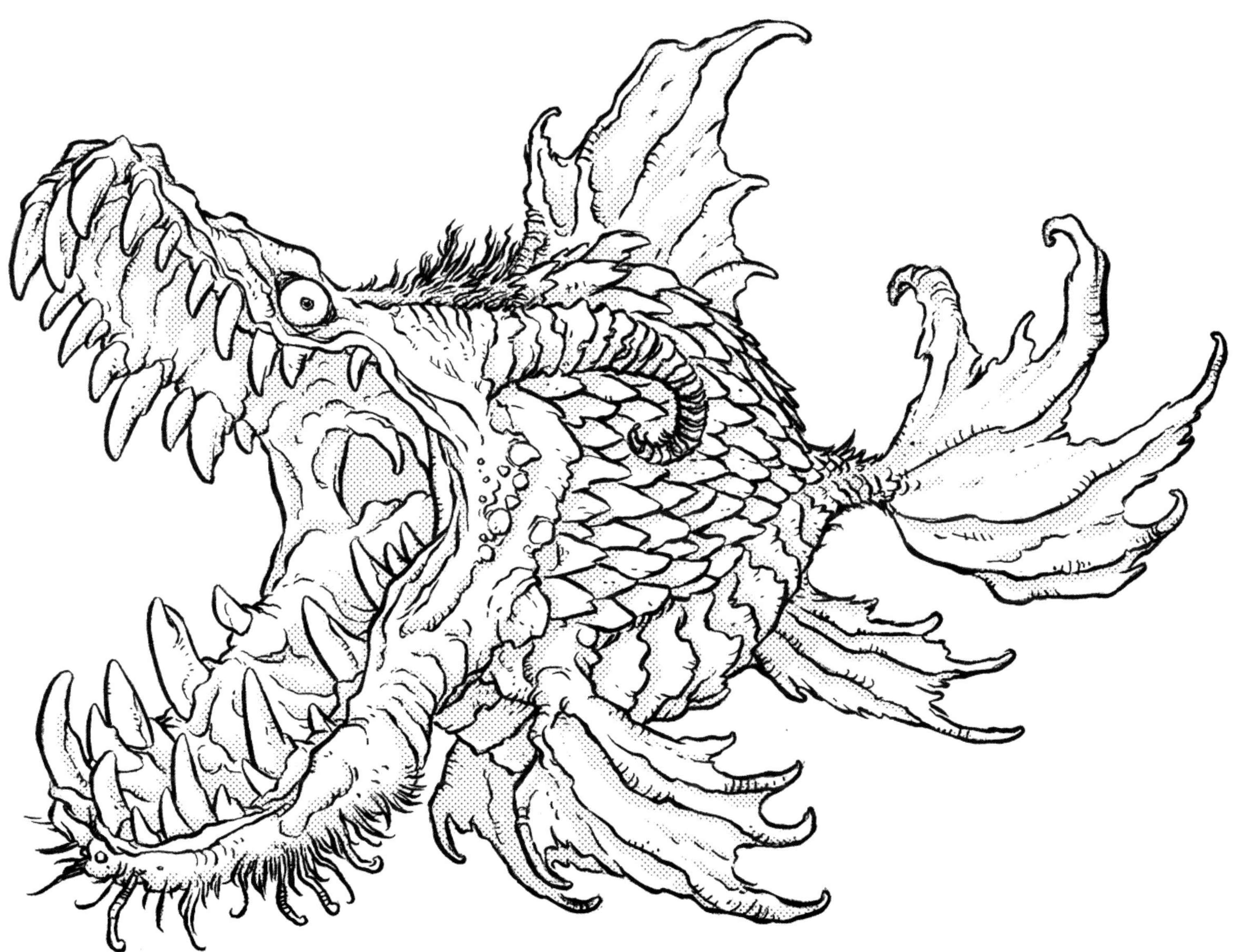

ARMORED SWEEPER FISH

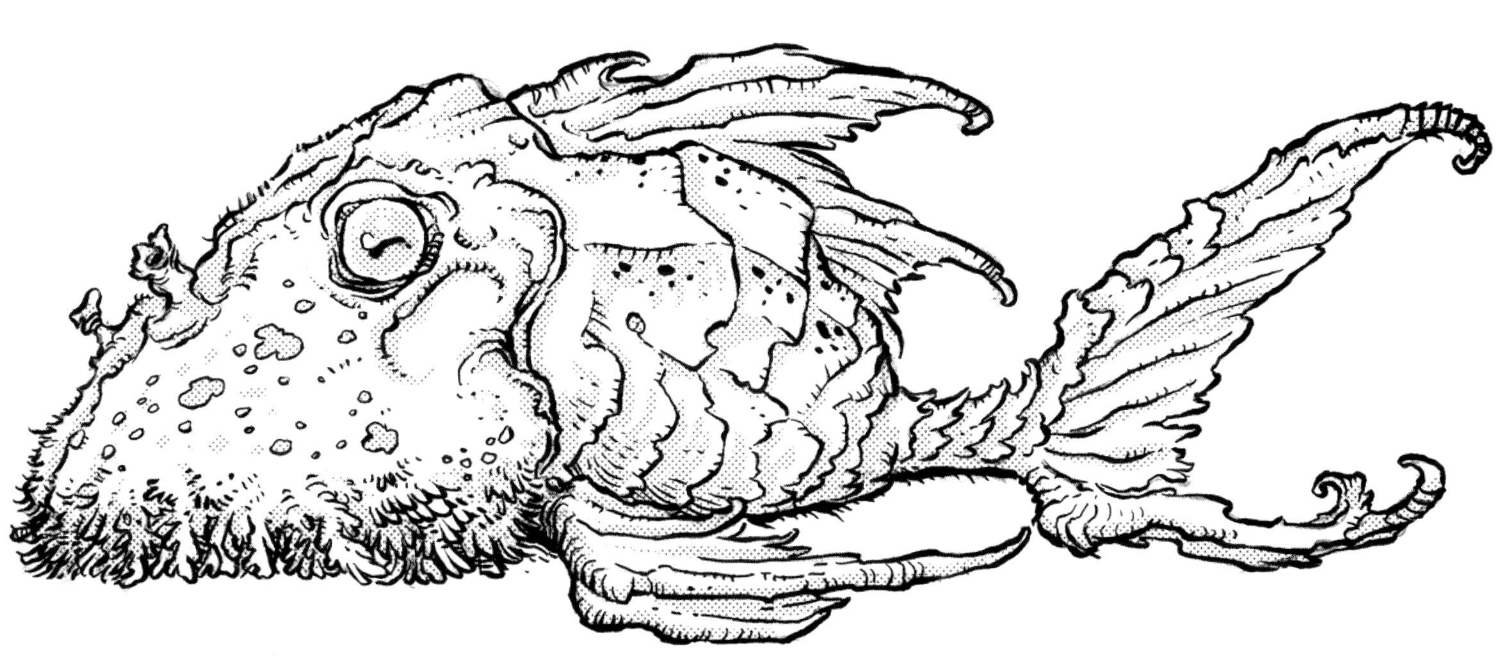

STIFF FIN DORKFISH

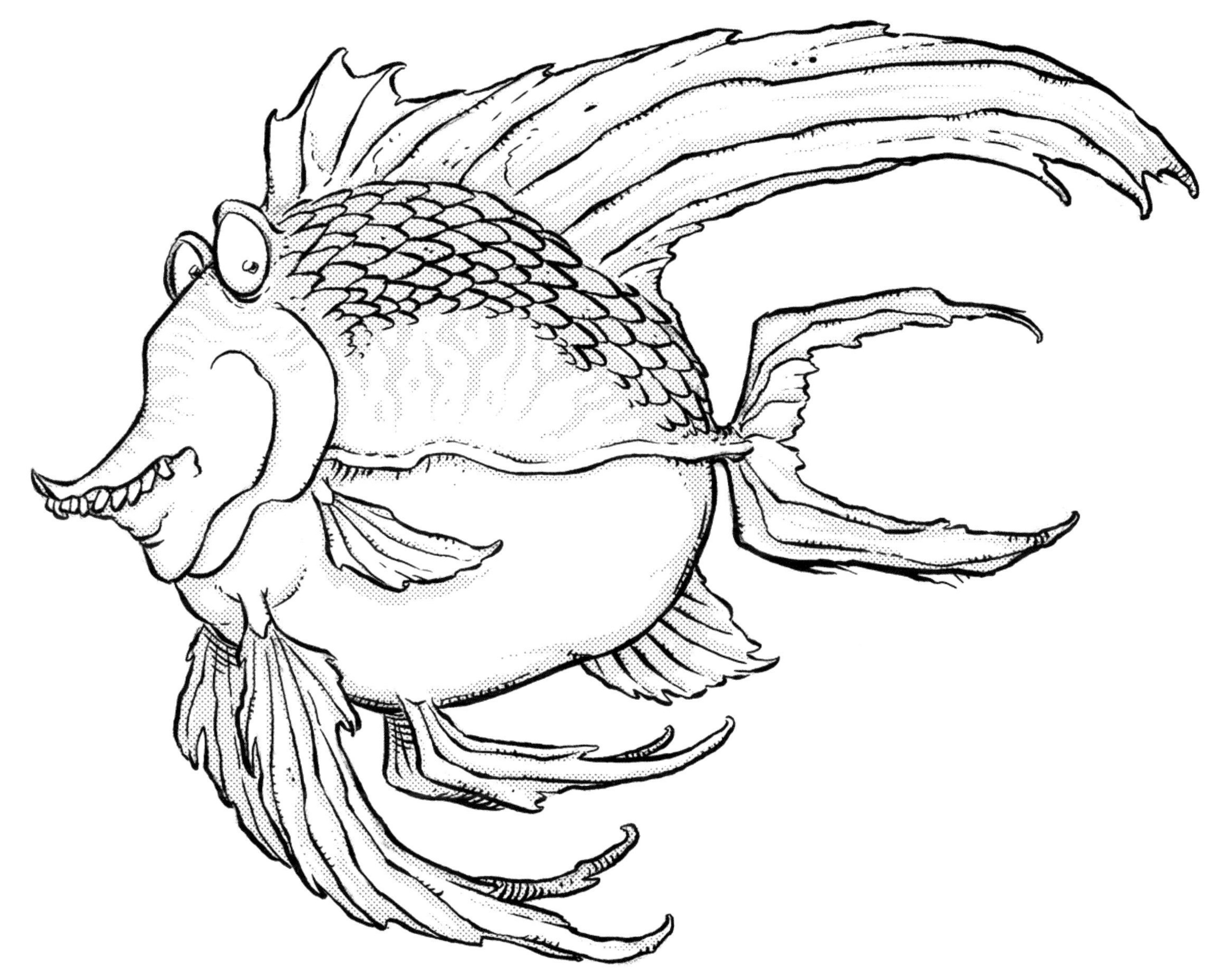

LONG-SNOUTED ZOMBIE FISH

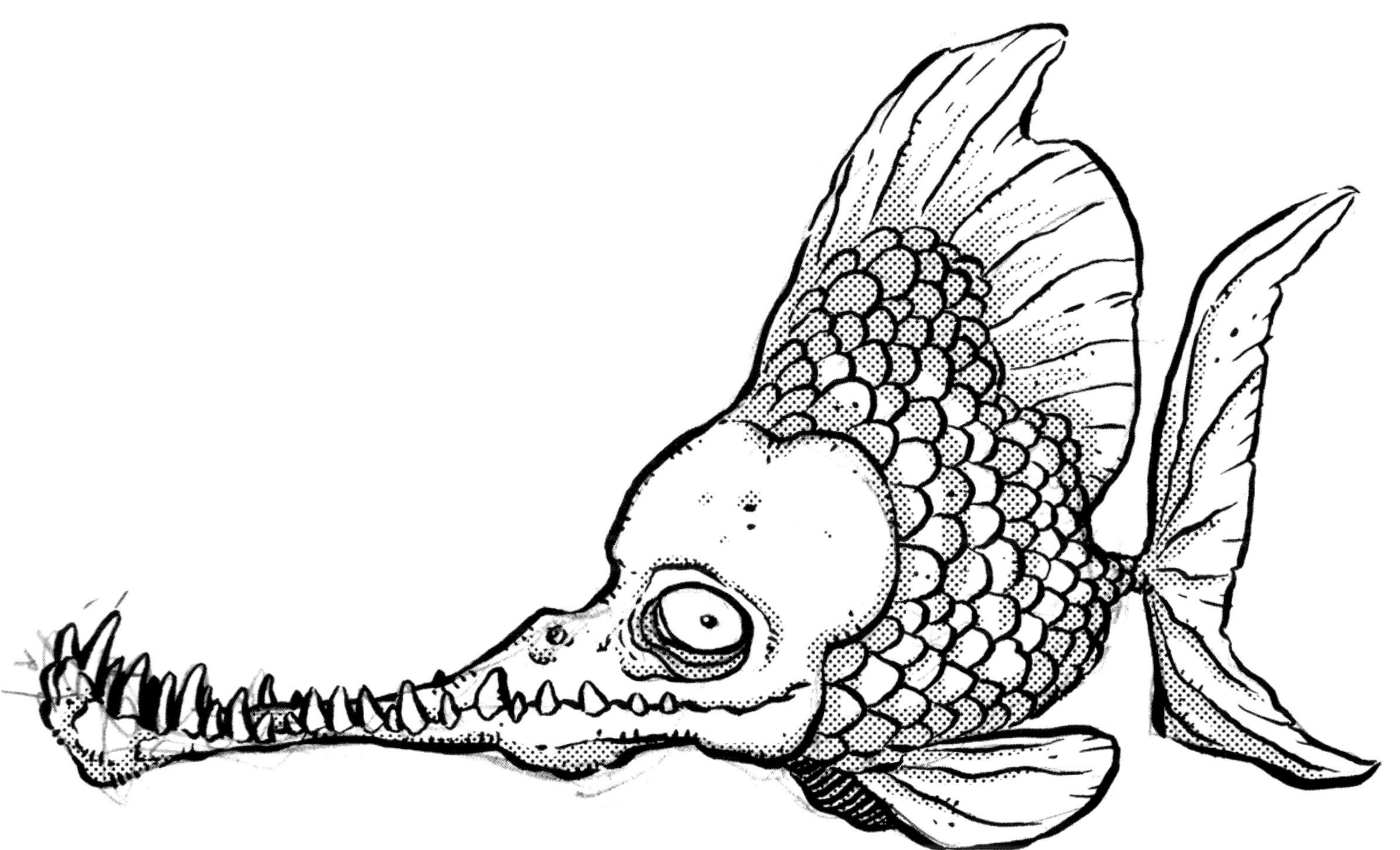

BANDED FANGSNOUT

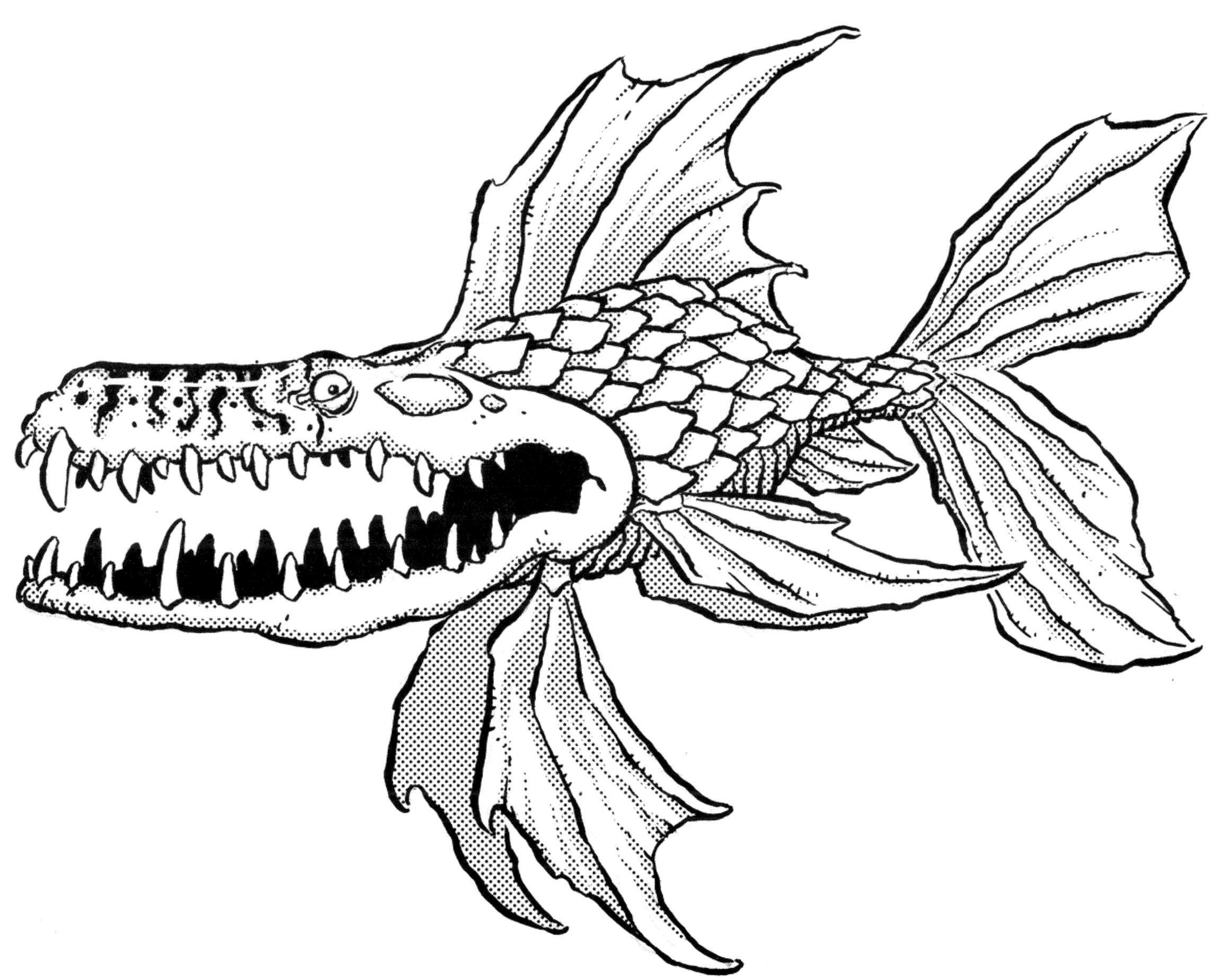

BEARDED SHOVELTOOTH

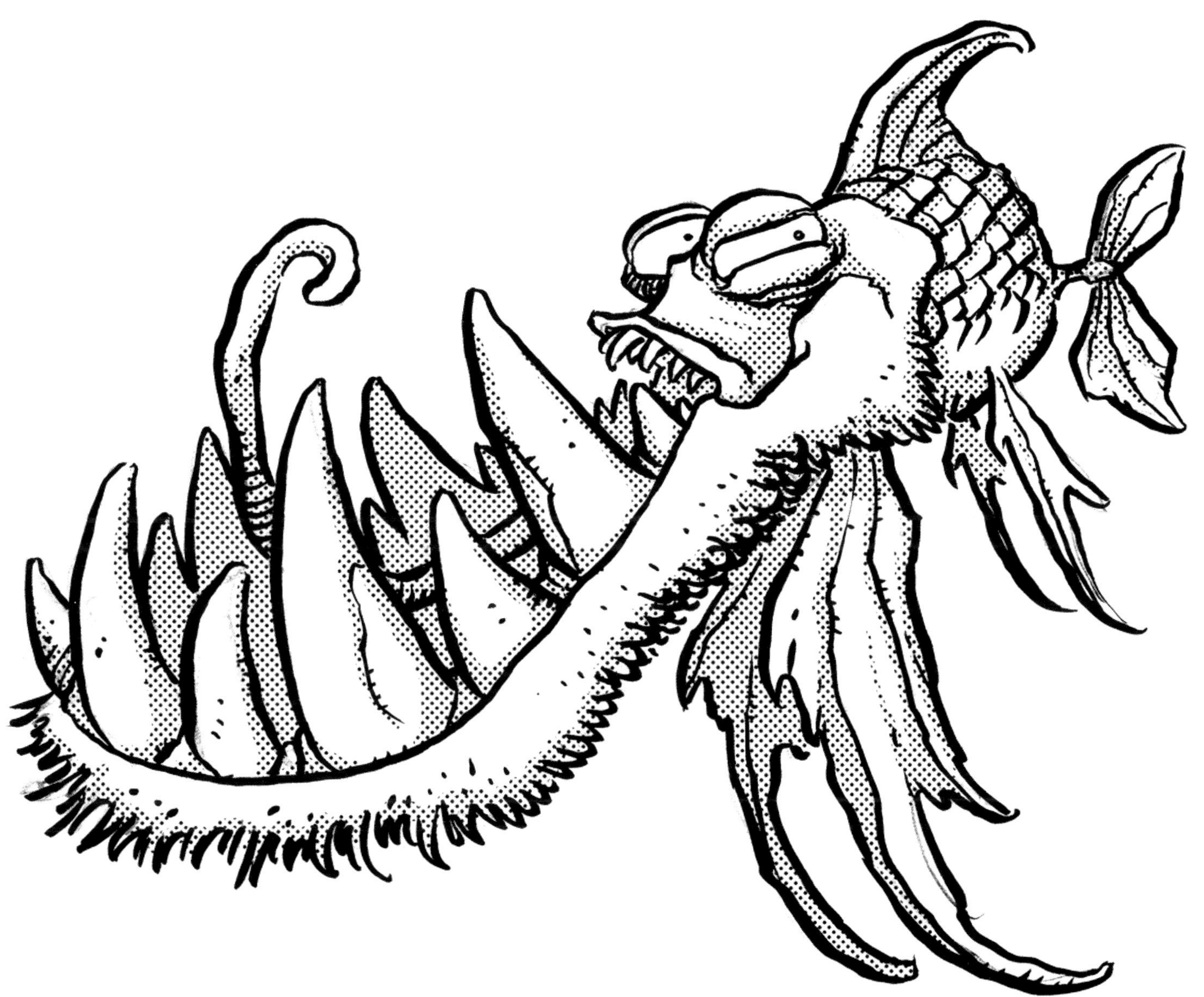

SPINDLY BIG GULP

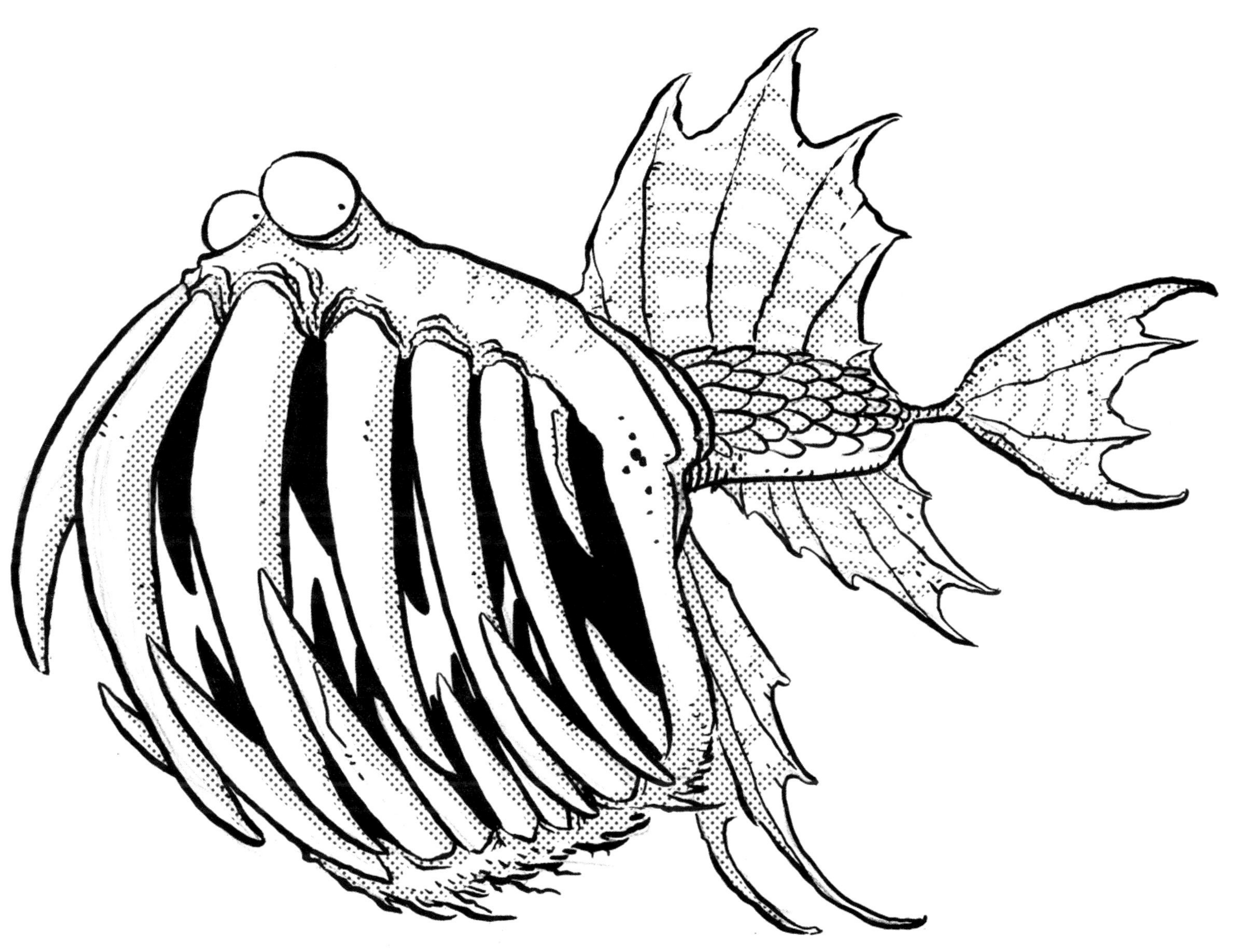

BIGJAW SCRUFF FISH

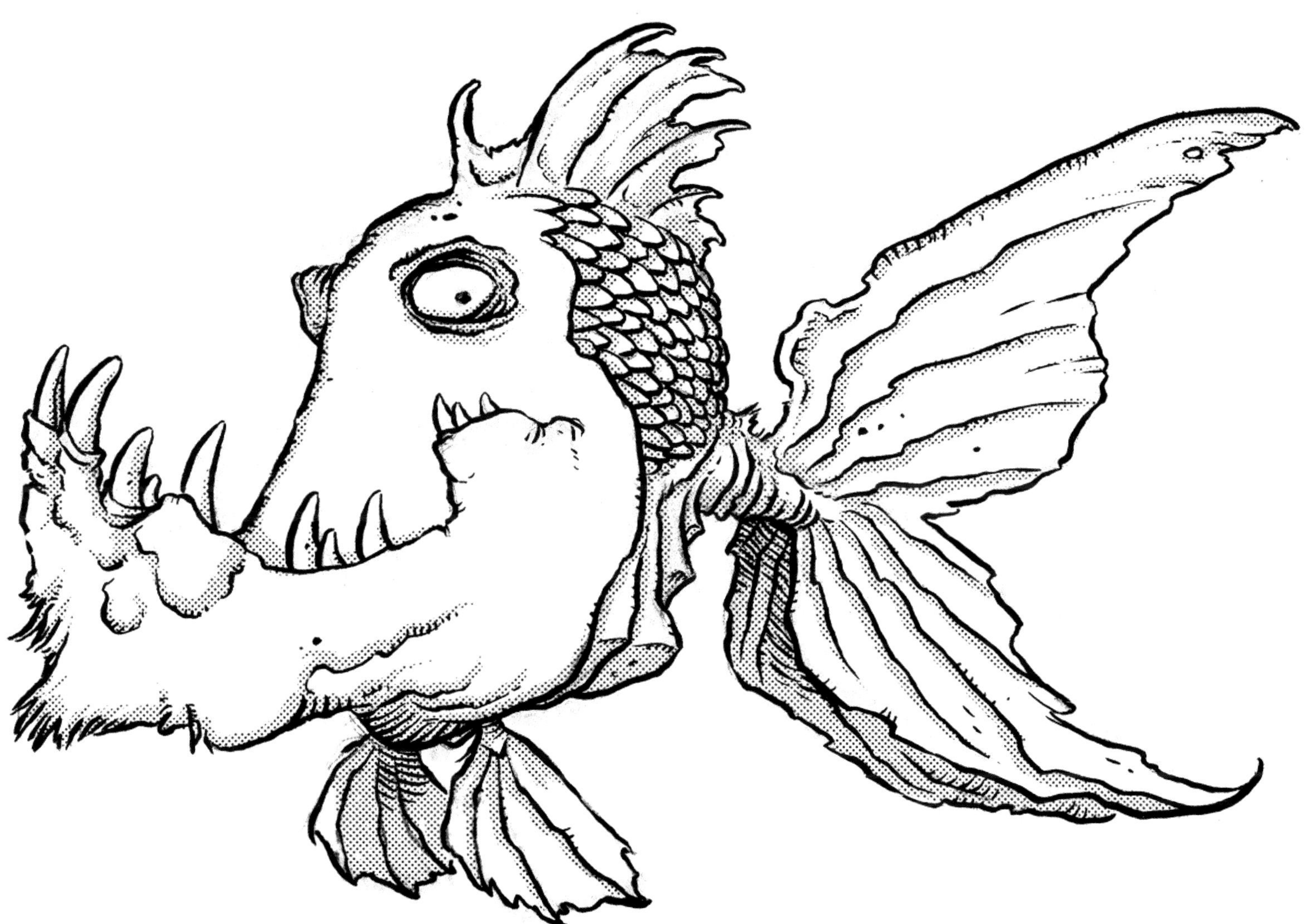

WHISKERED CRESCENT-HEAD

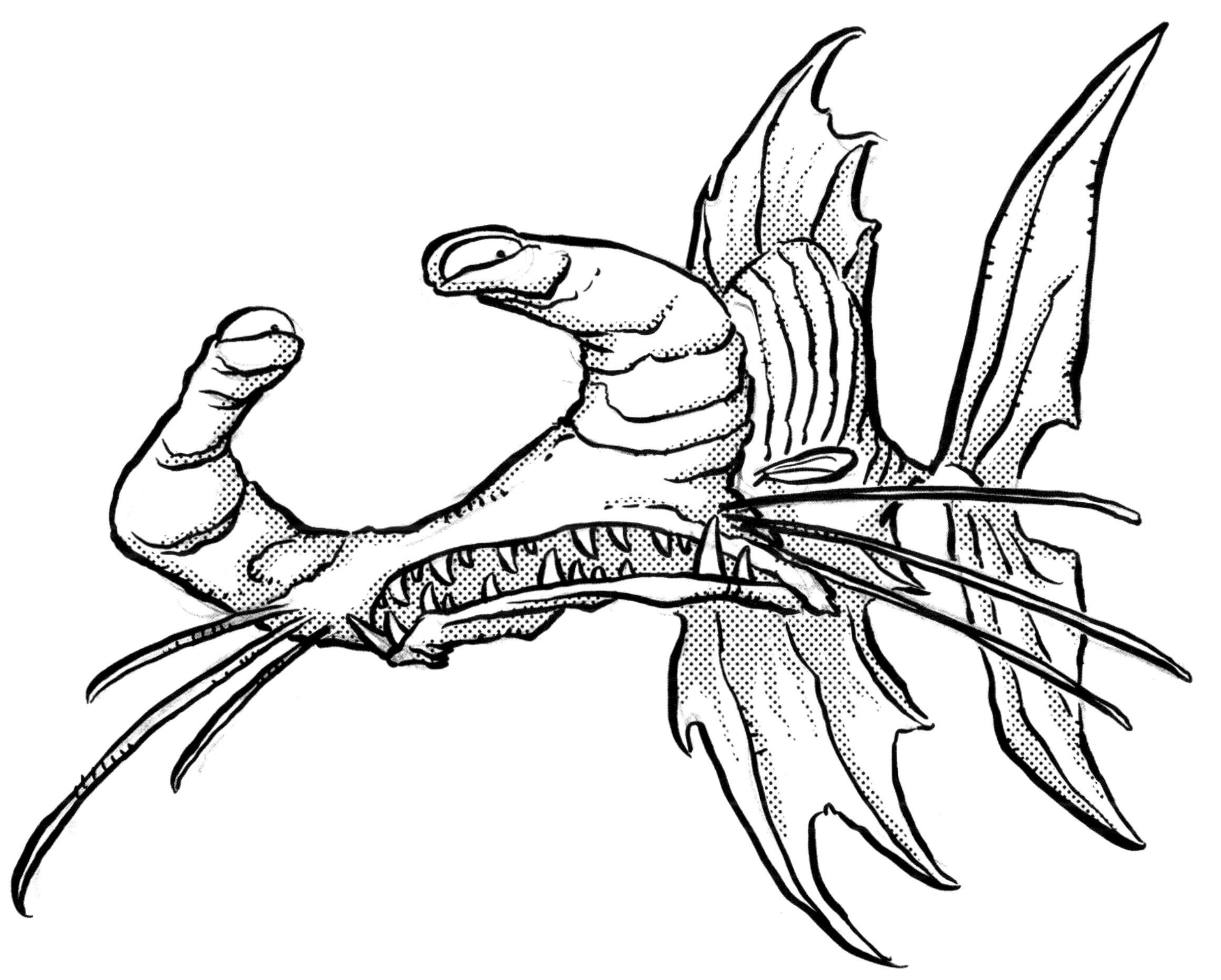

STUDDED RIDGEHEAD

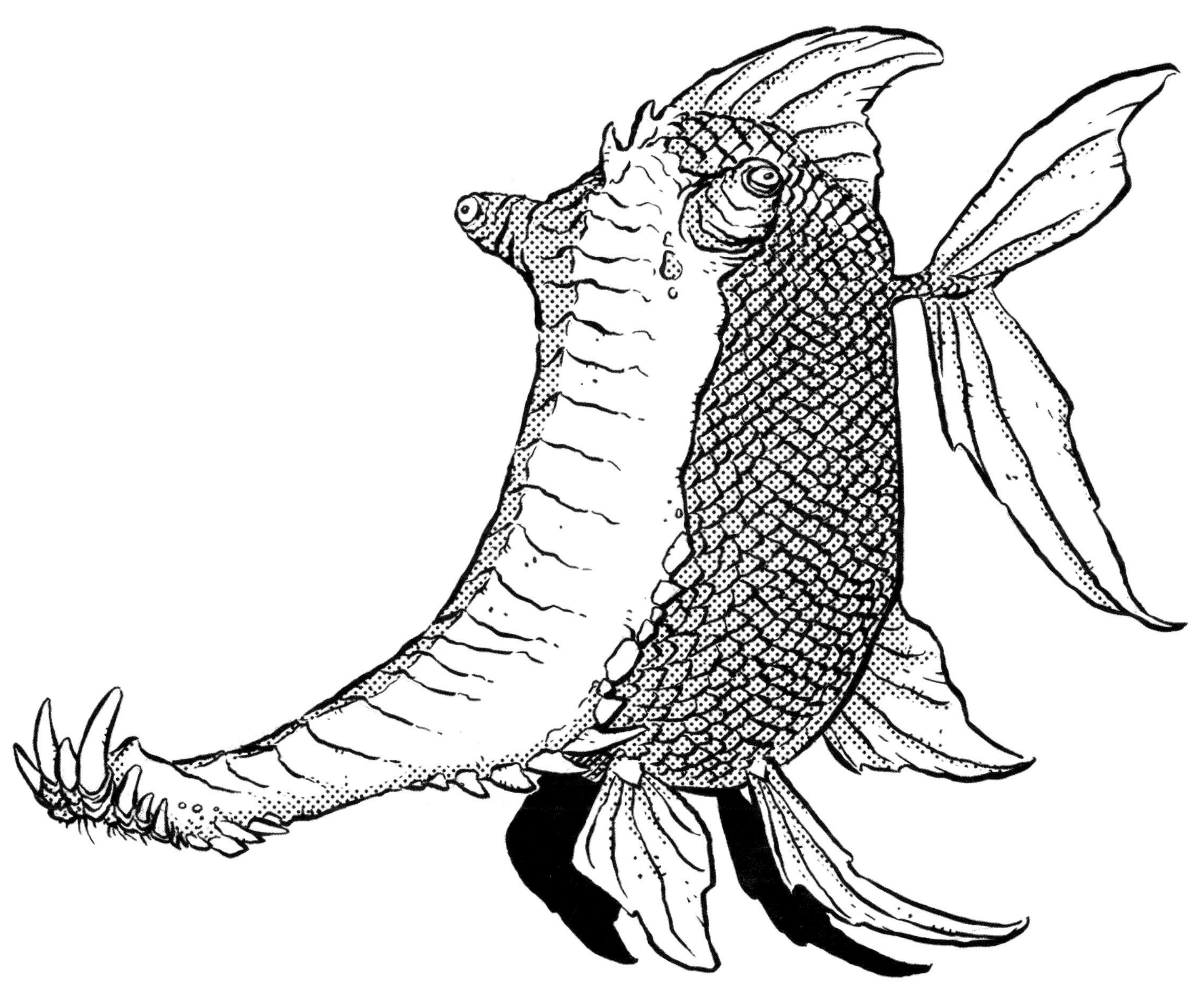

CENTURY FISH

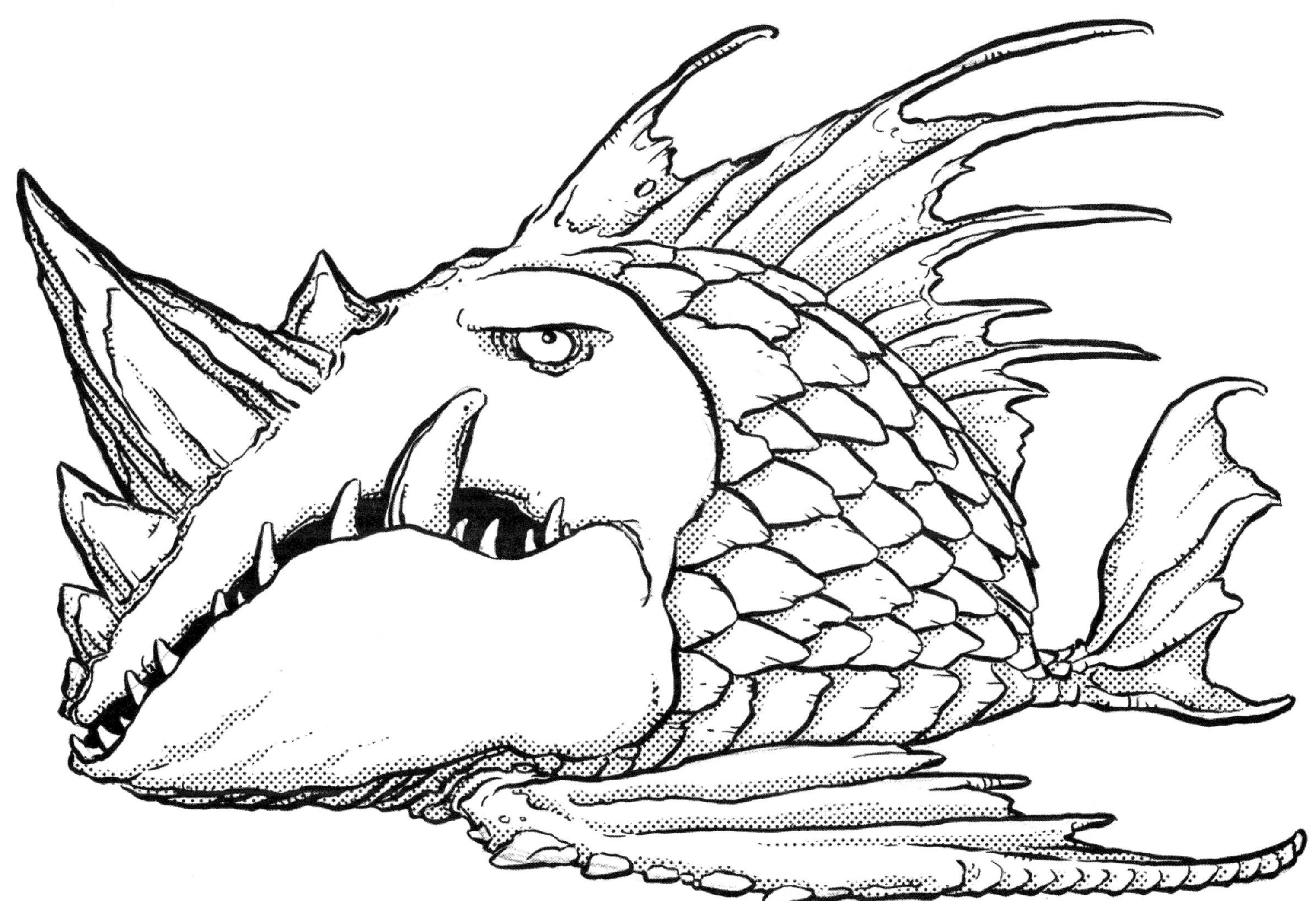

BURROWING DRAGON FISH

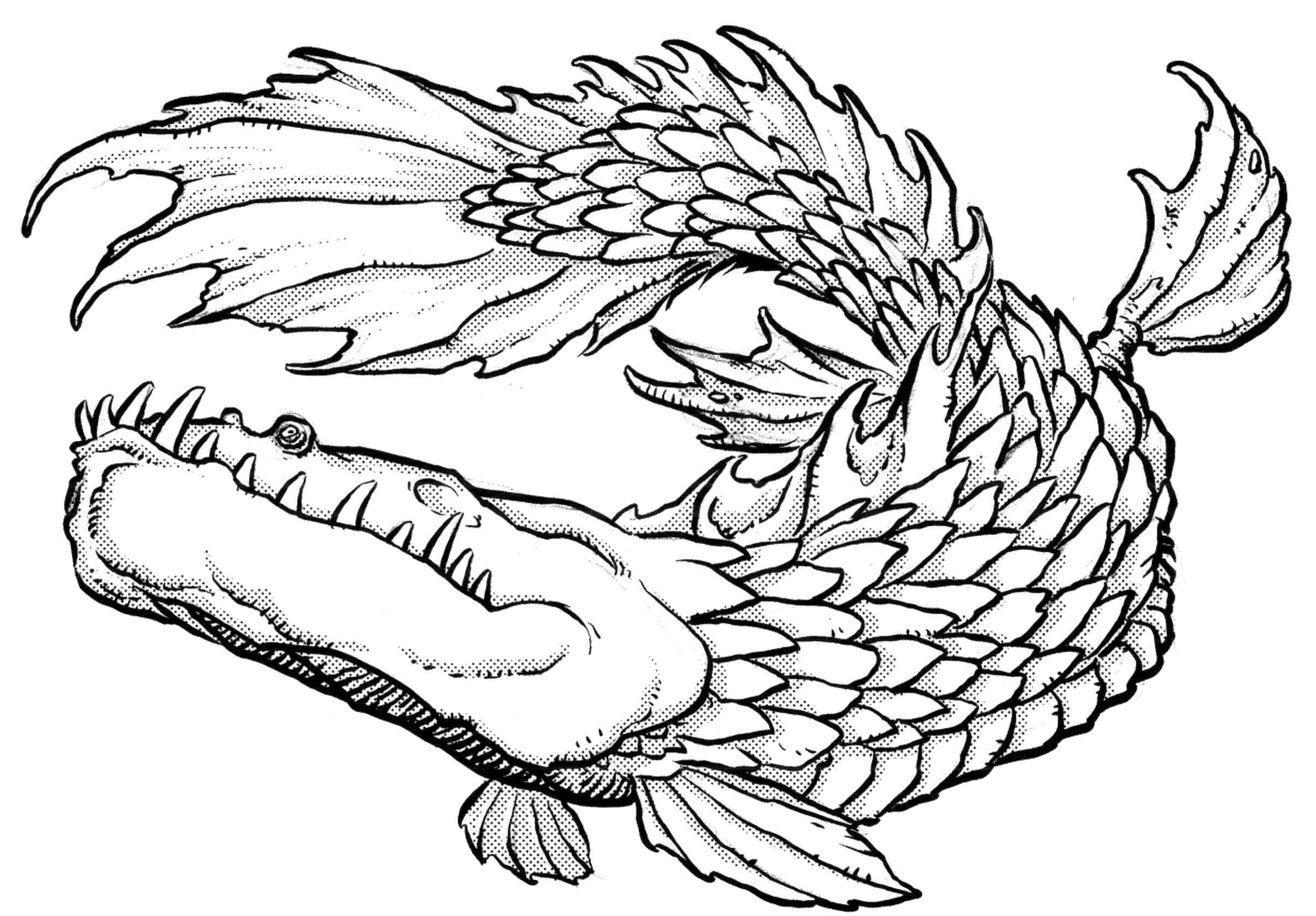

CLEFT-CHIN SNOOT FISH

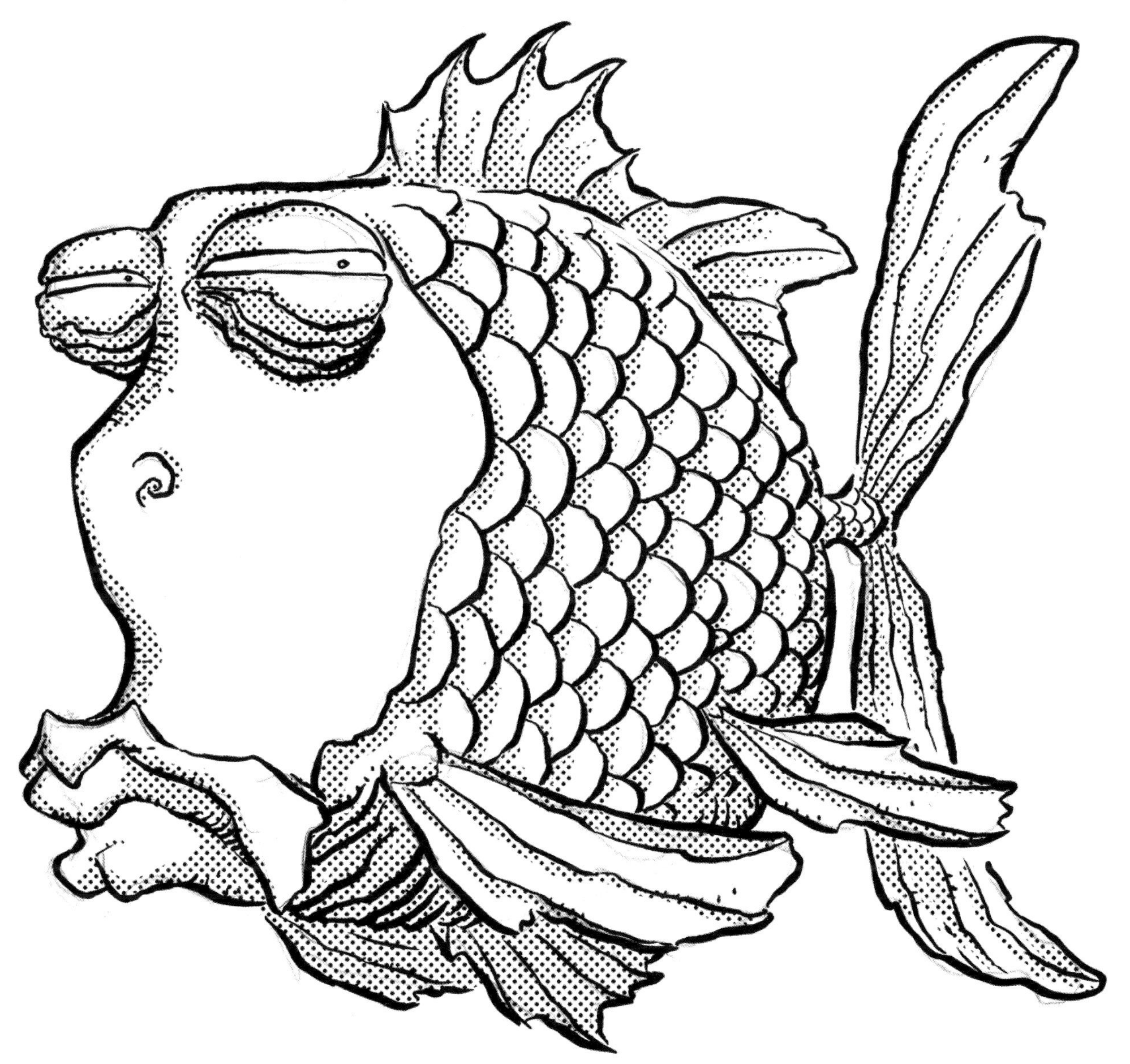

LONGFACE

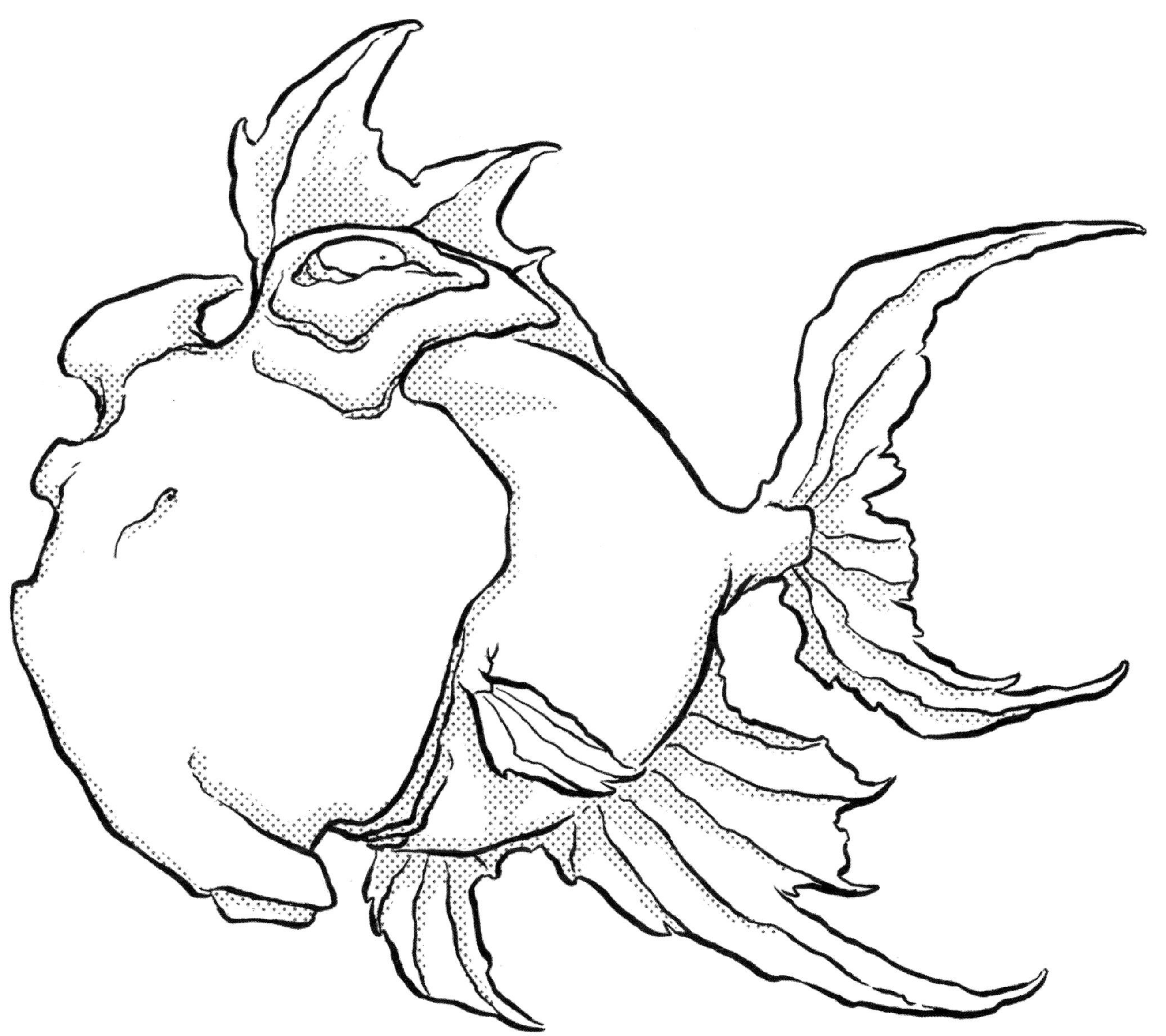

GARAGE SALE FISH

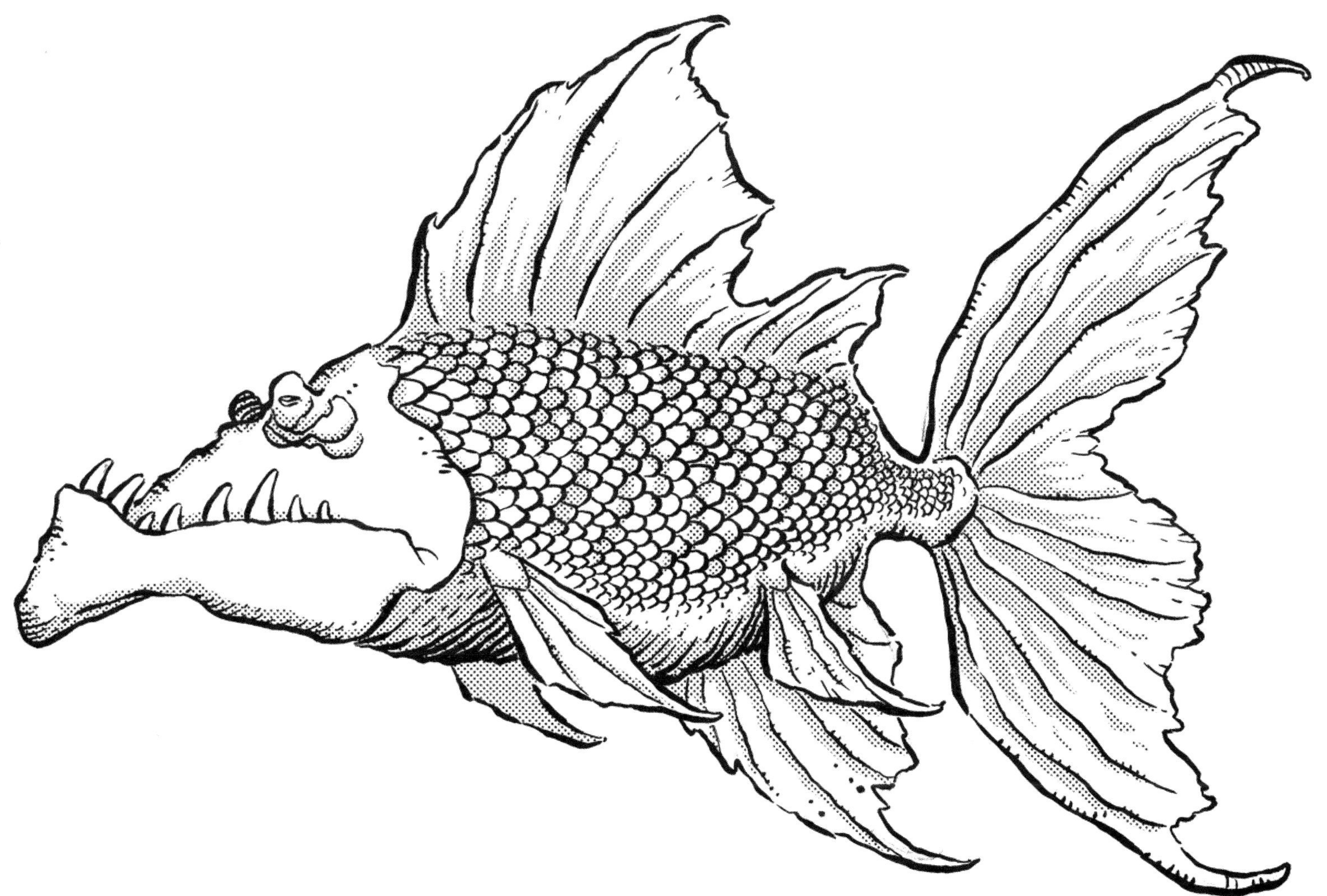

IGOR FISH

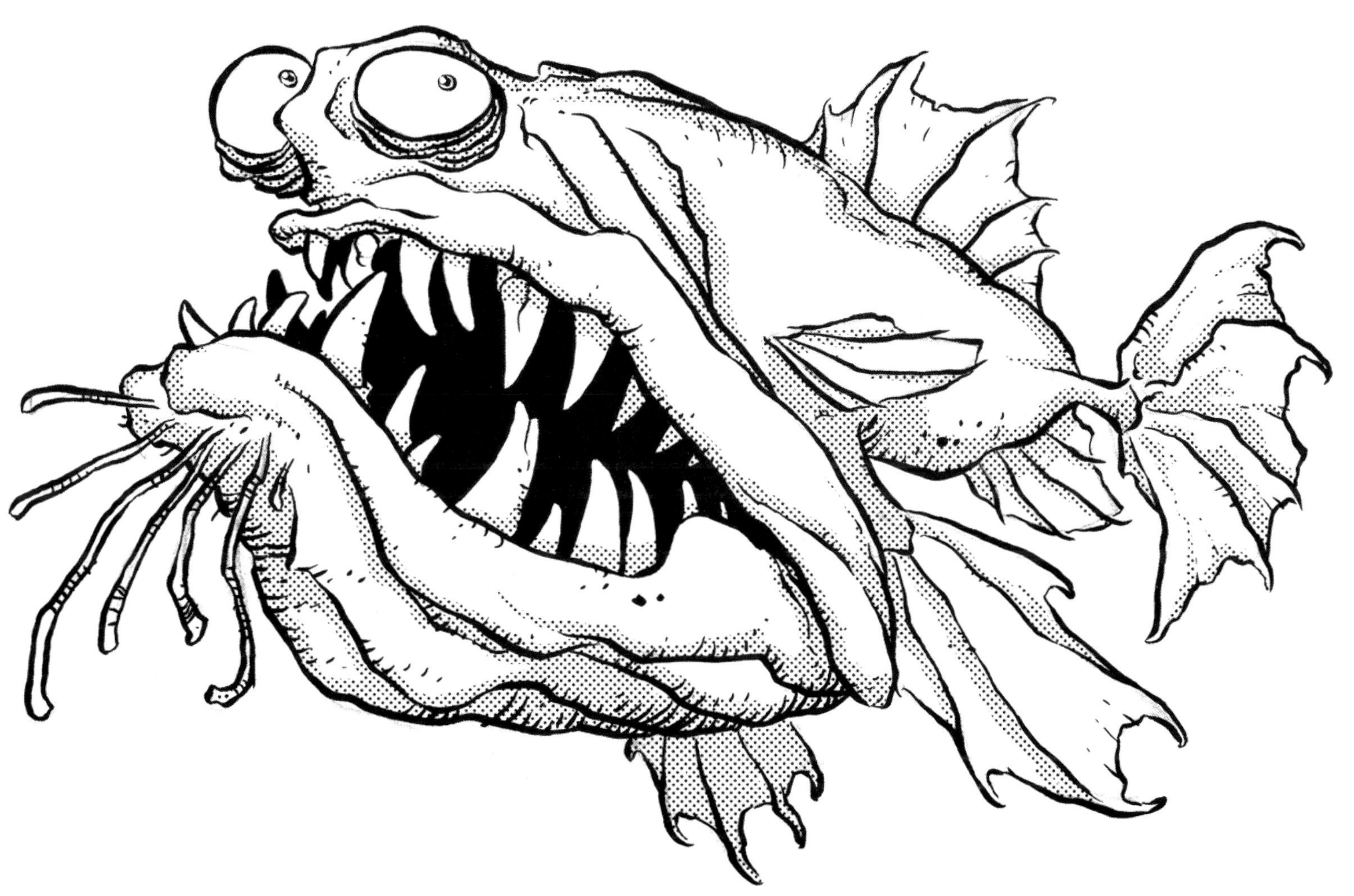

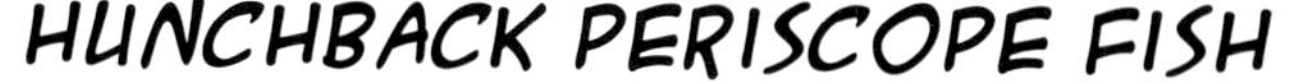
HUNCHBACK PERISCOPE FISH

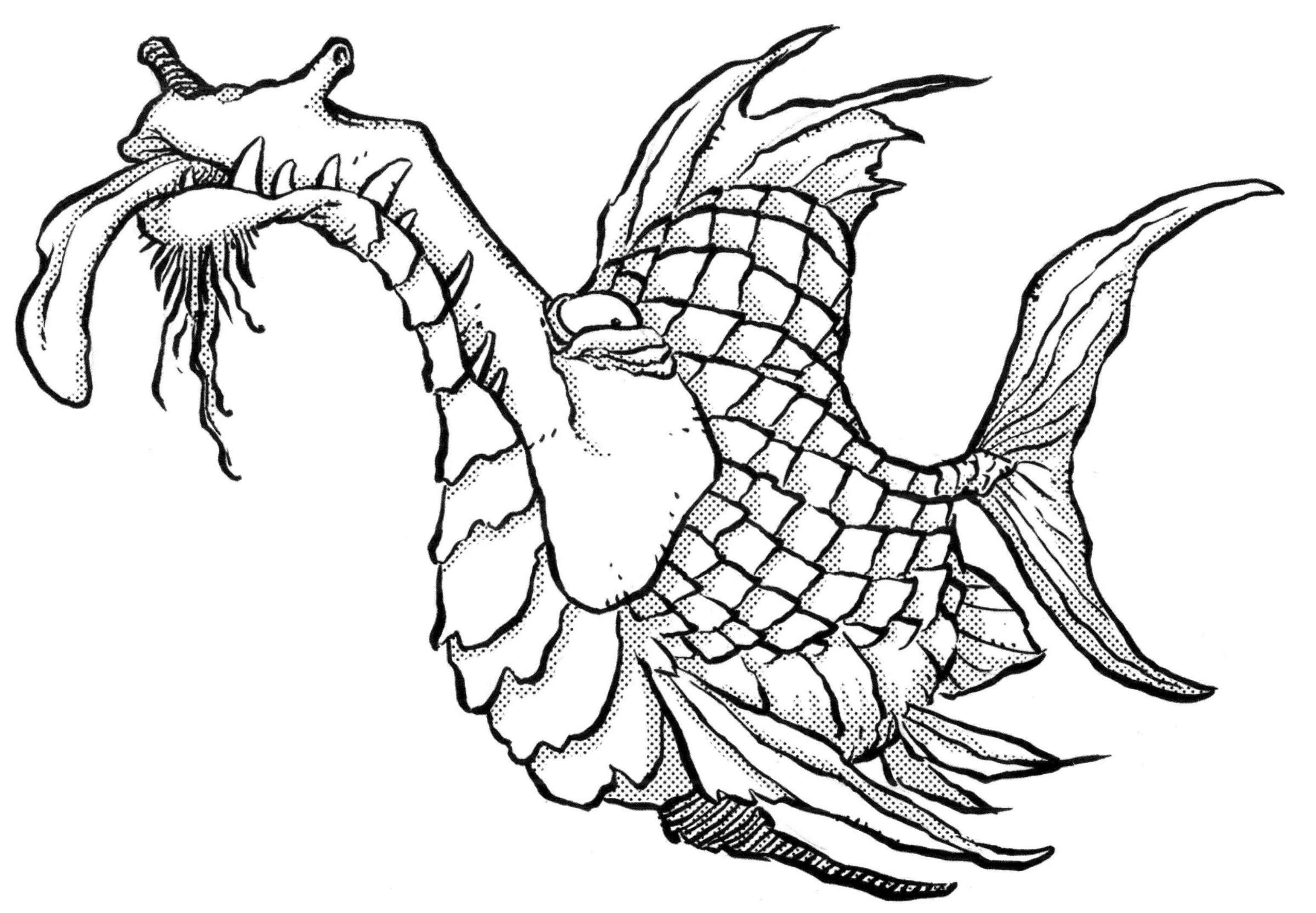

HEADLAMP MAW FISH

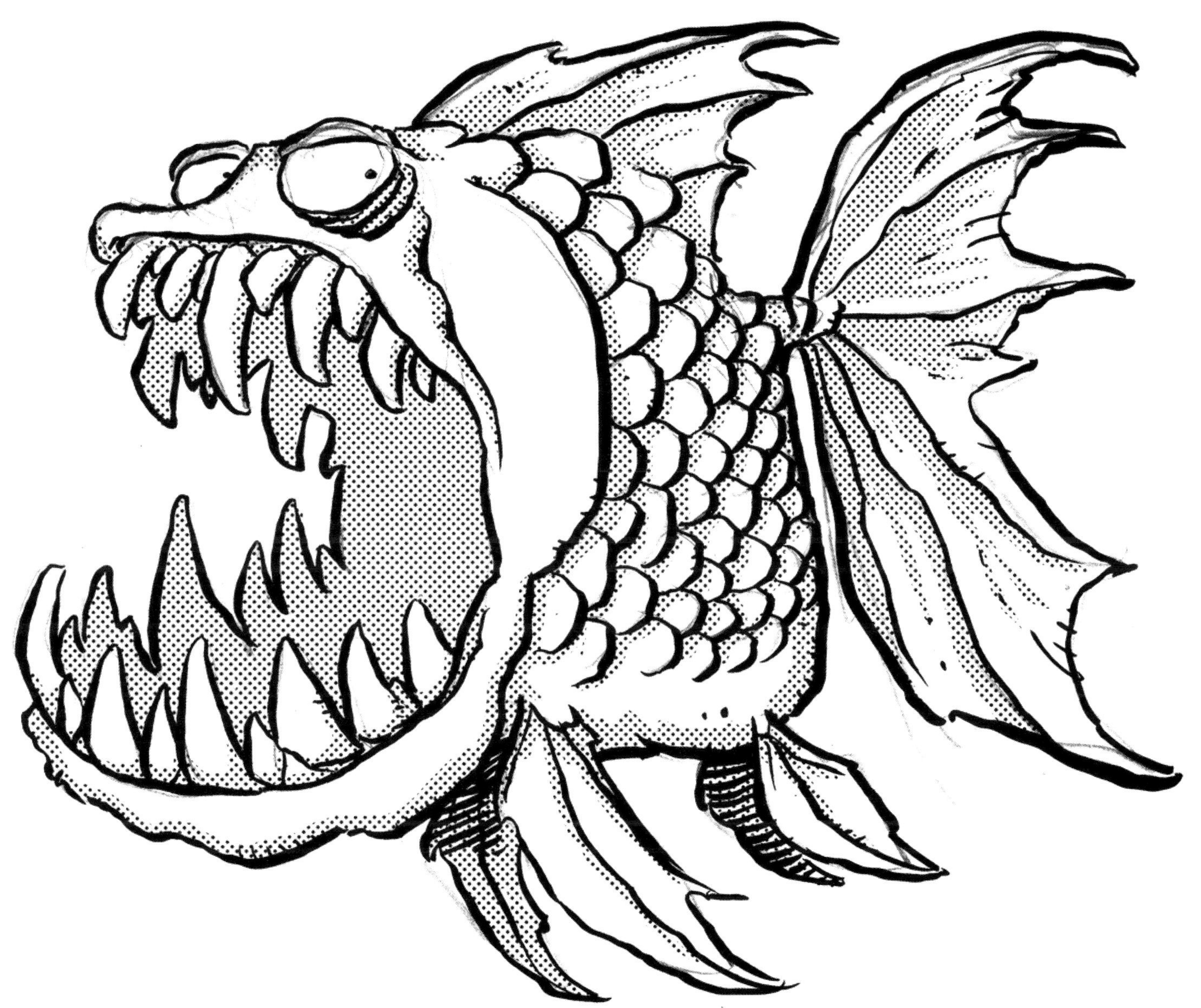

FRIDAY THE 13TH FISH

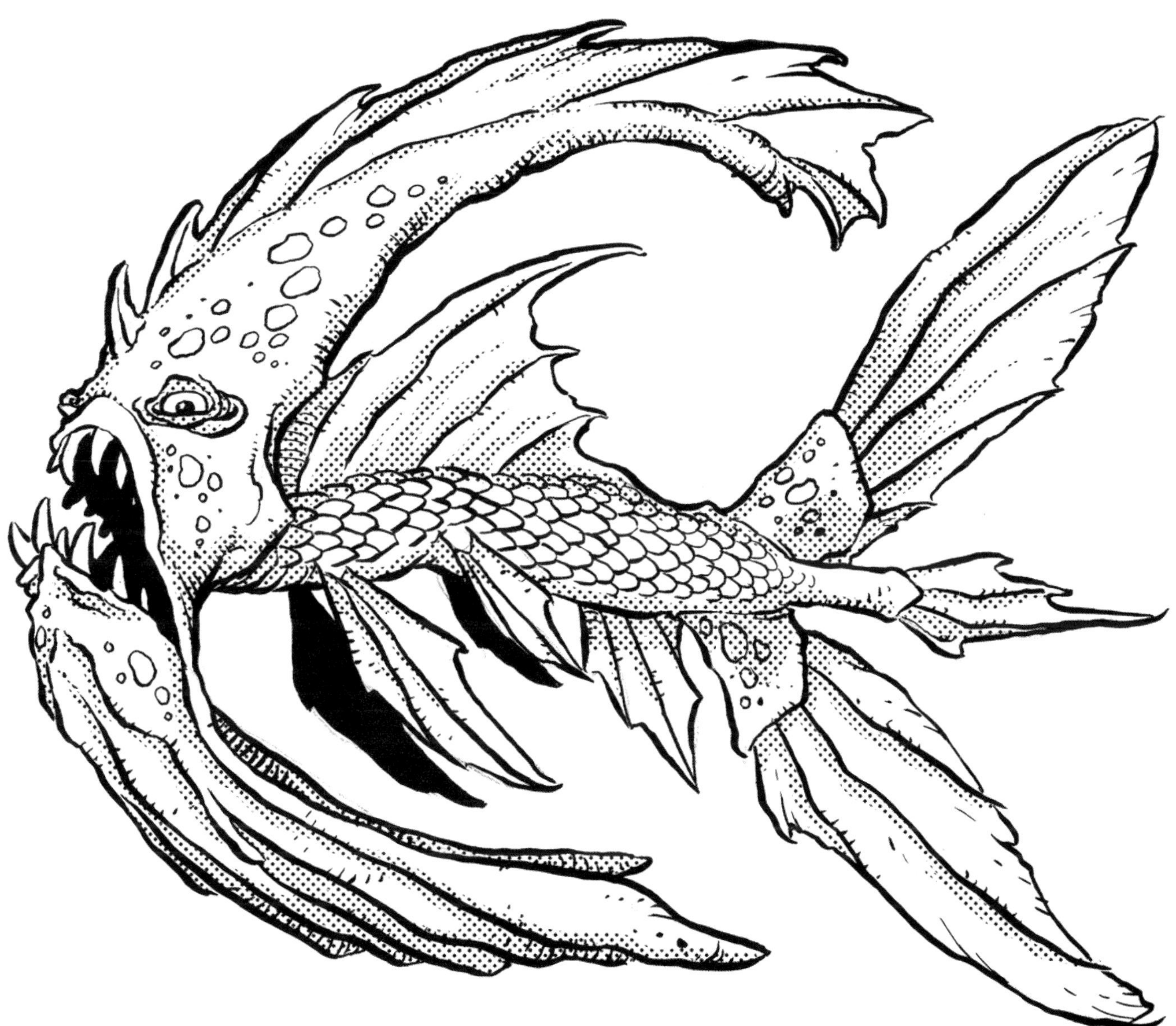

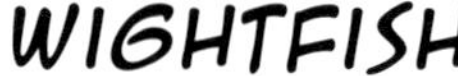
WIGHTFISH

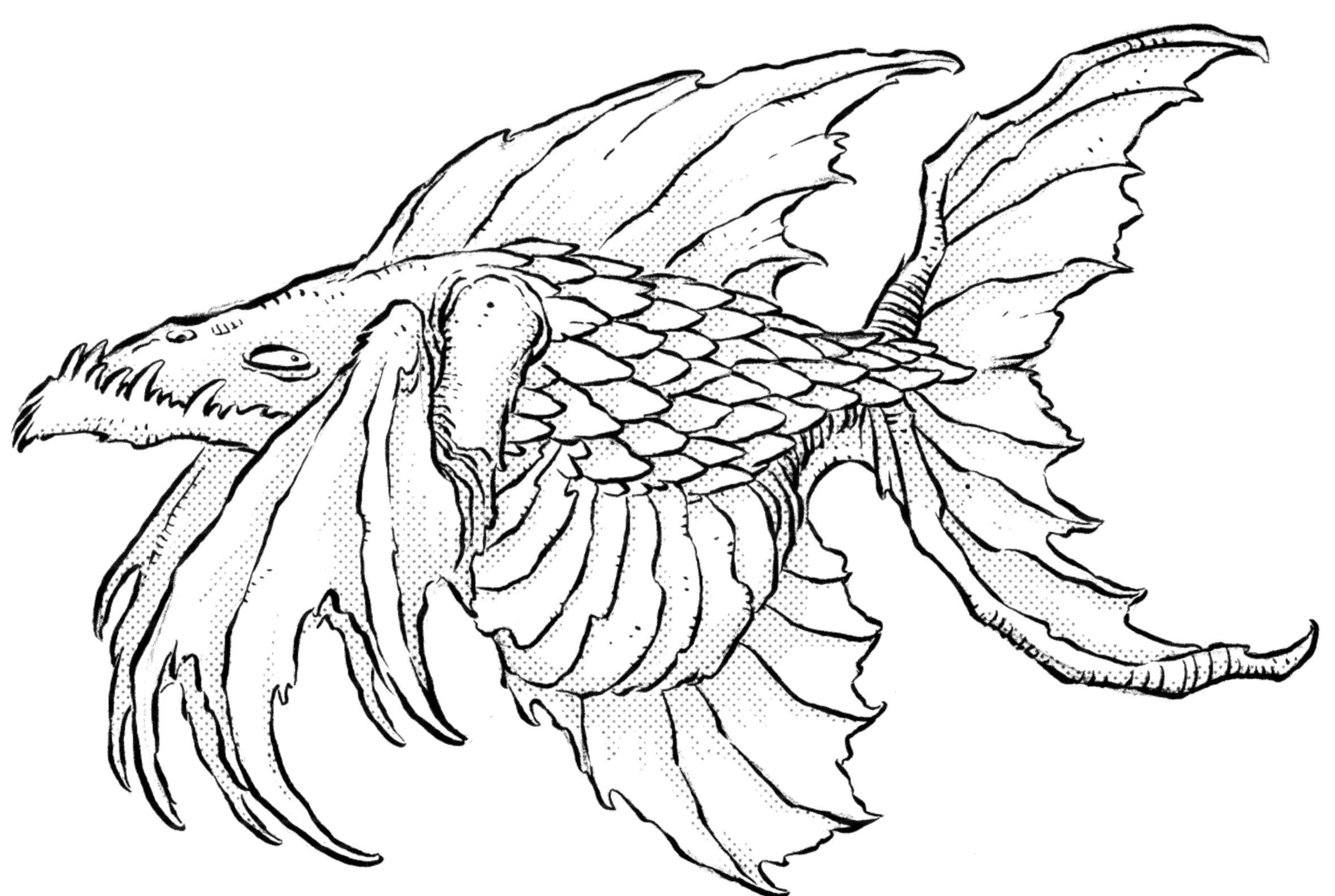

WARTY SPURTAIL

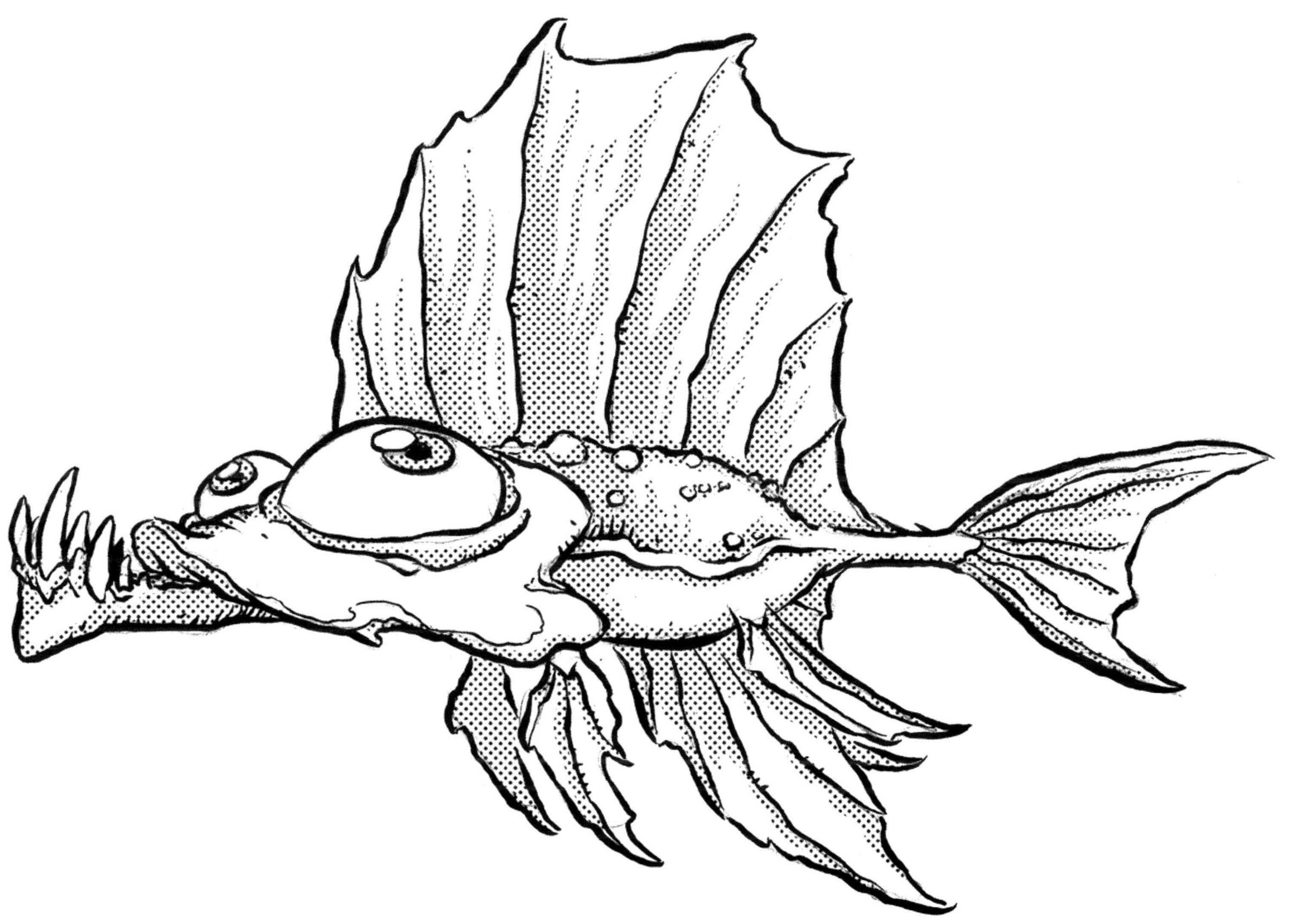

SEGMENTED BROOMFISH

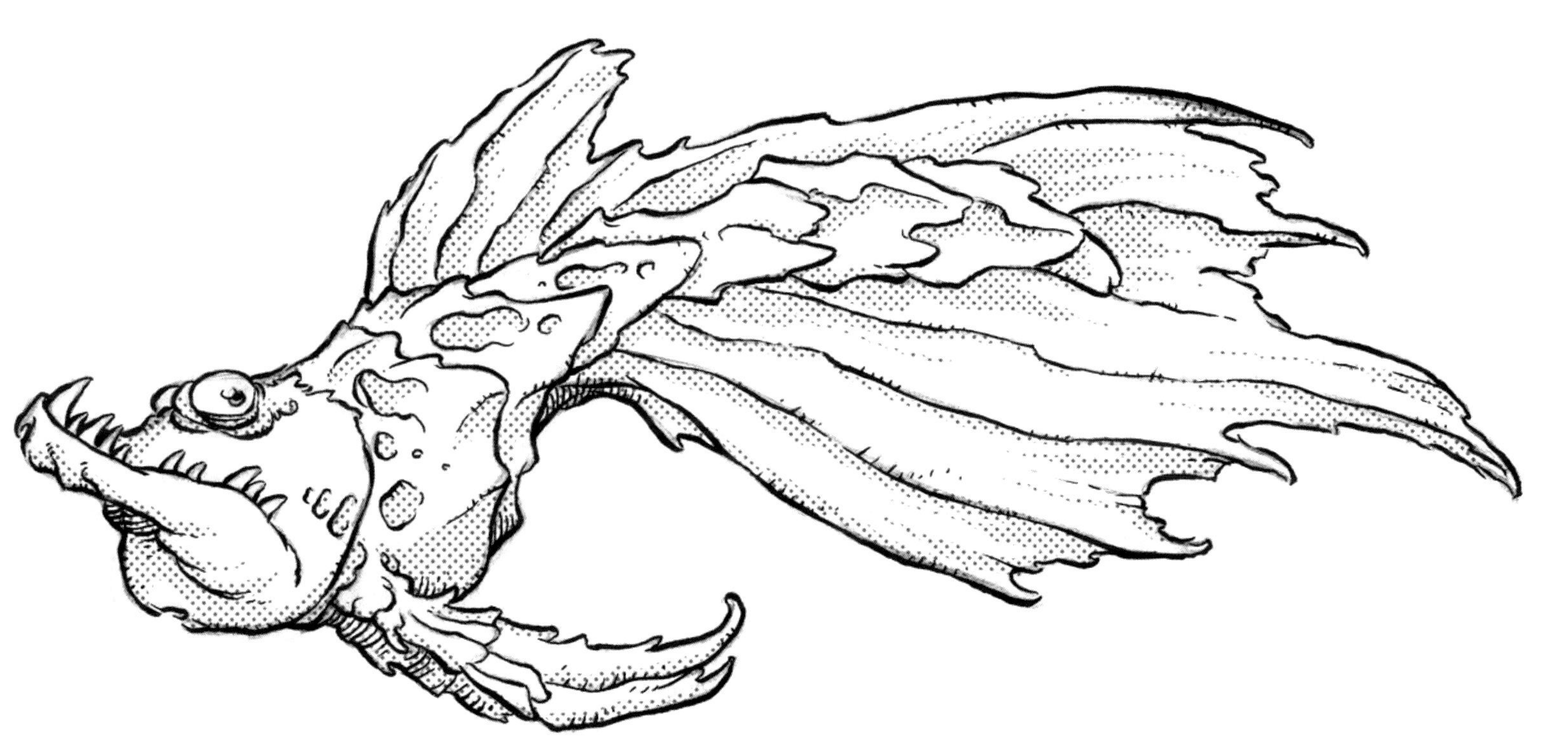

SPOTTED HORNED BELLYFISH

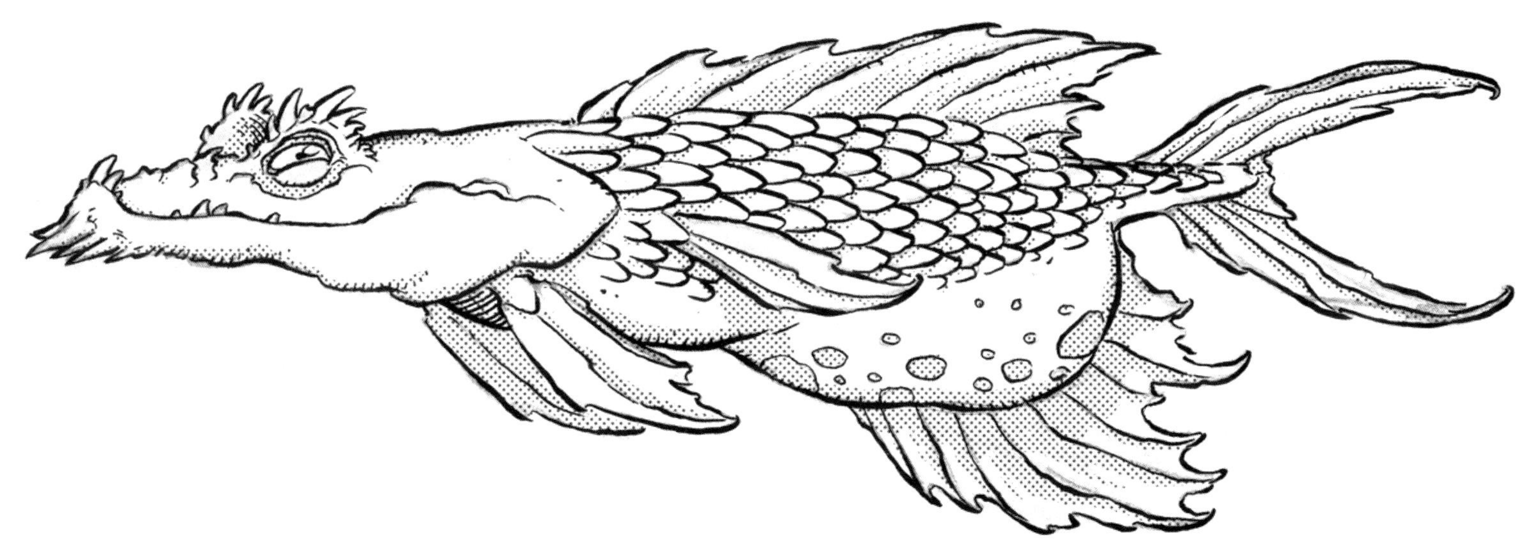

DRAWBRIDGE WALLEYE

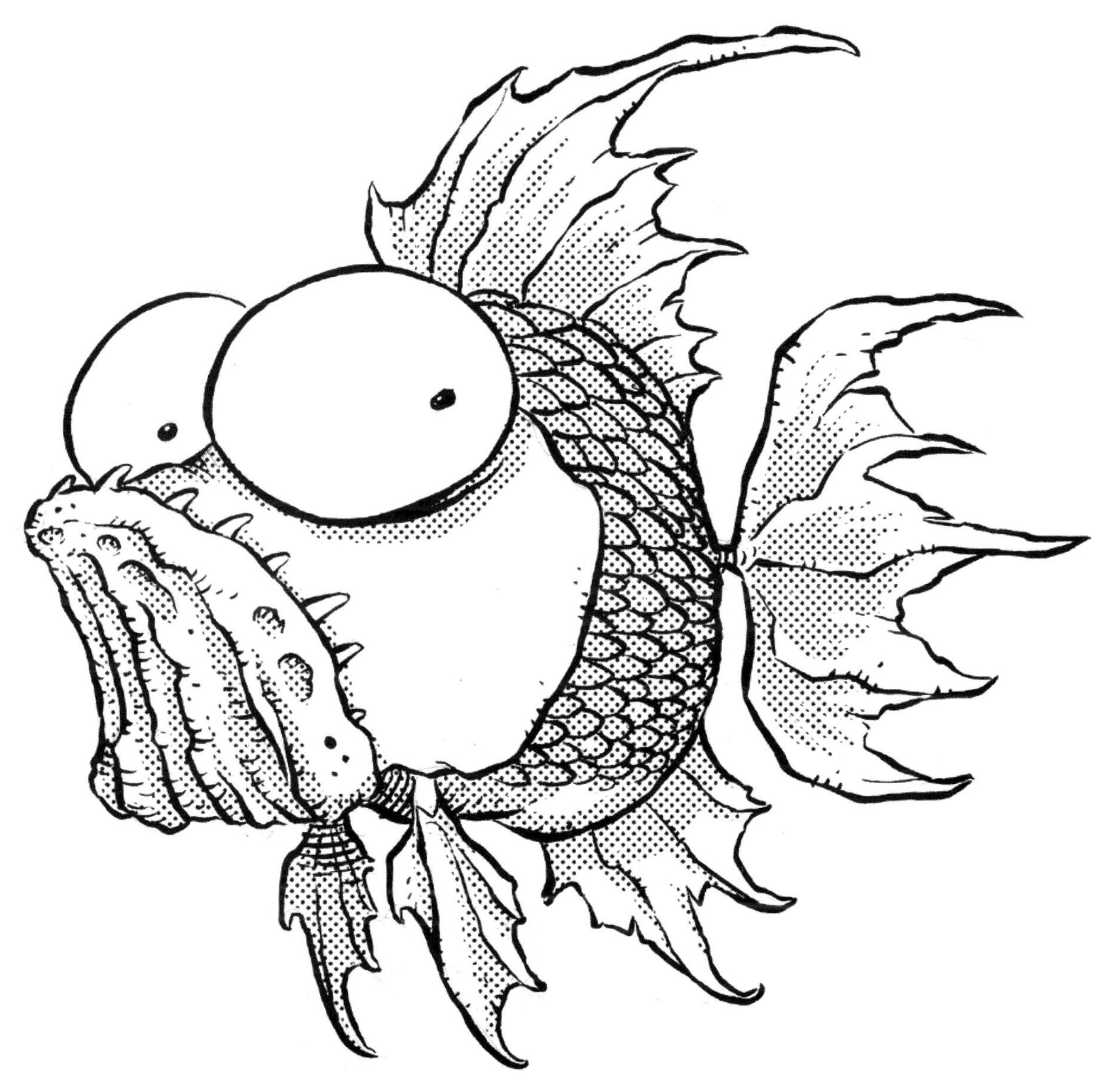

BLUNT BIGEYE

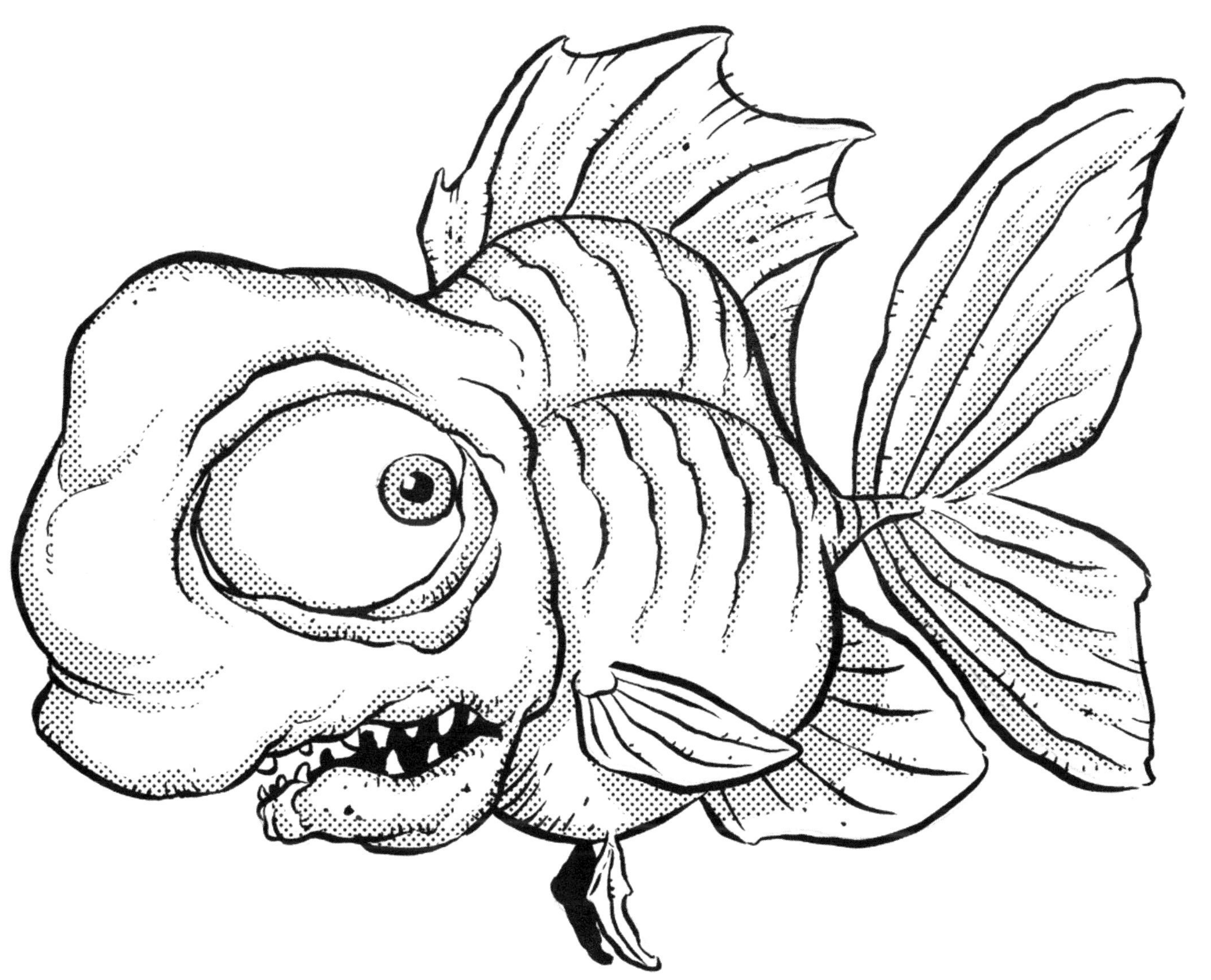

STUNTED BLACKTIP SHARK

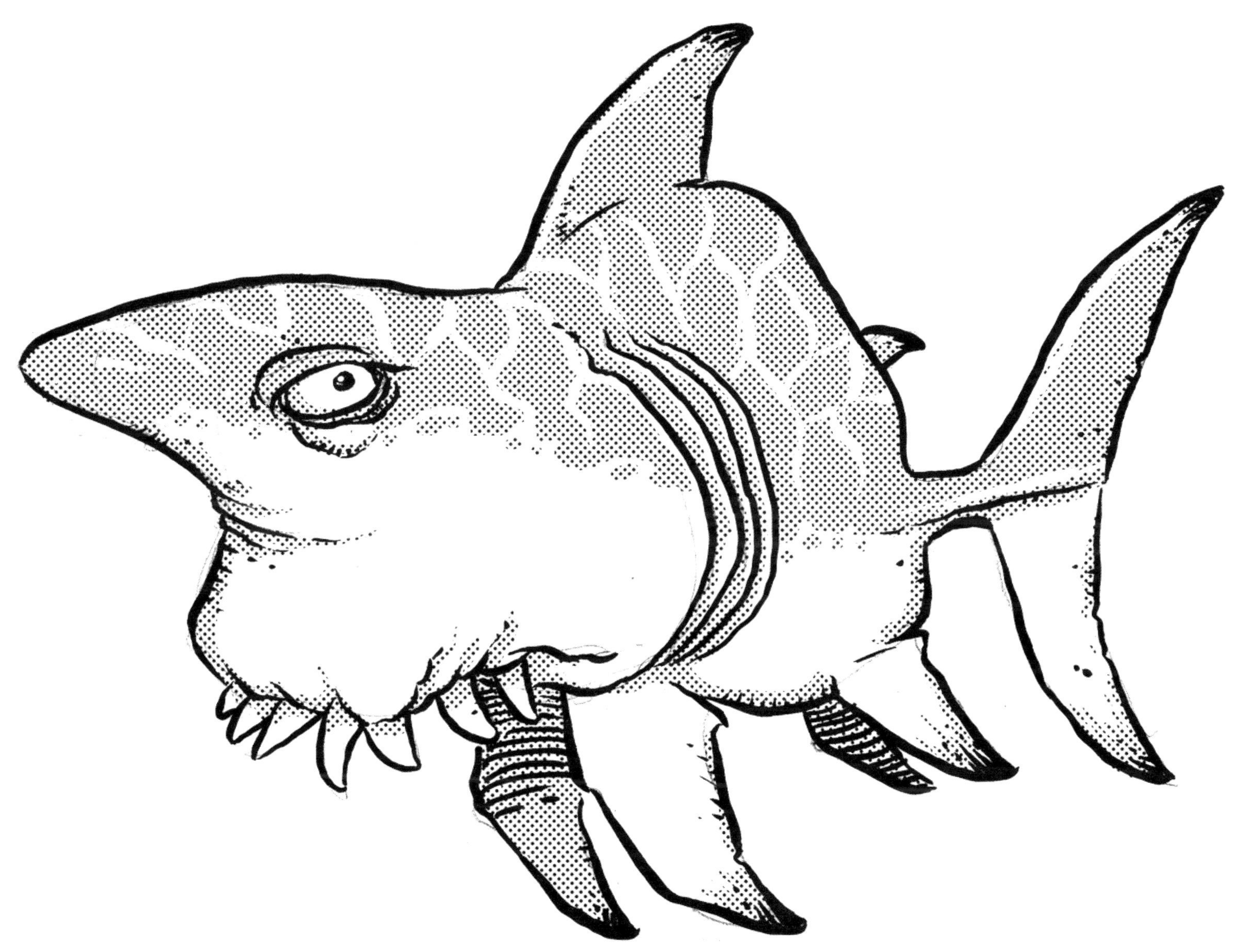

CHROMATIC LILYMOUTH

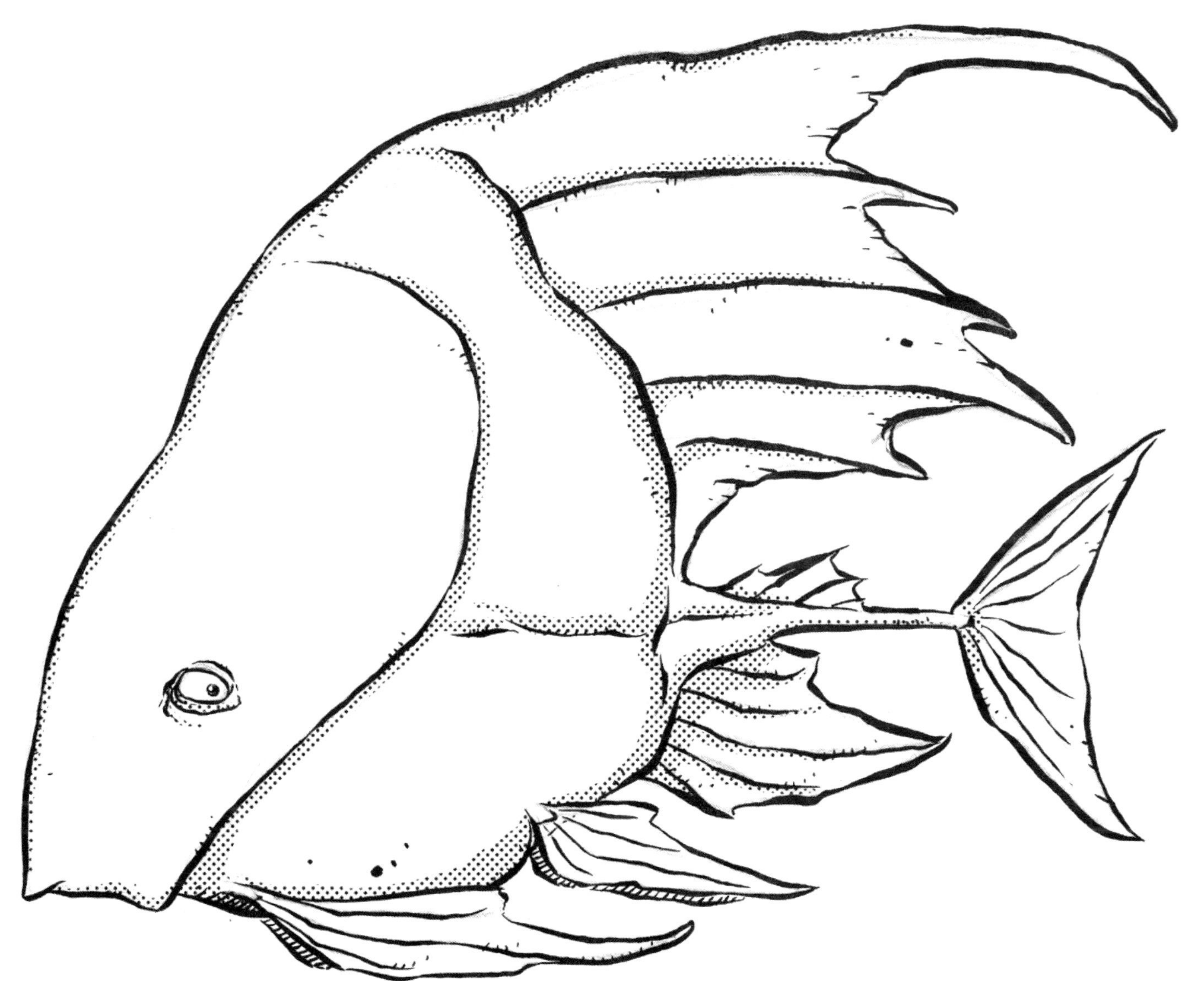

RETRIEVER GAR

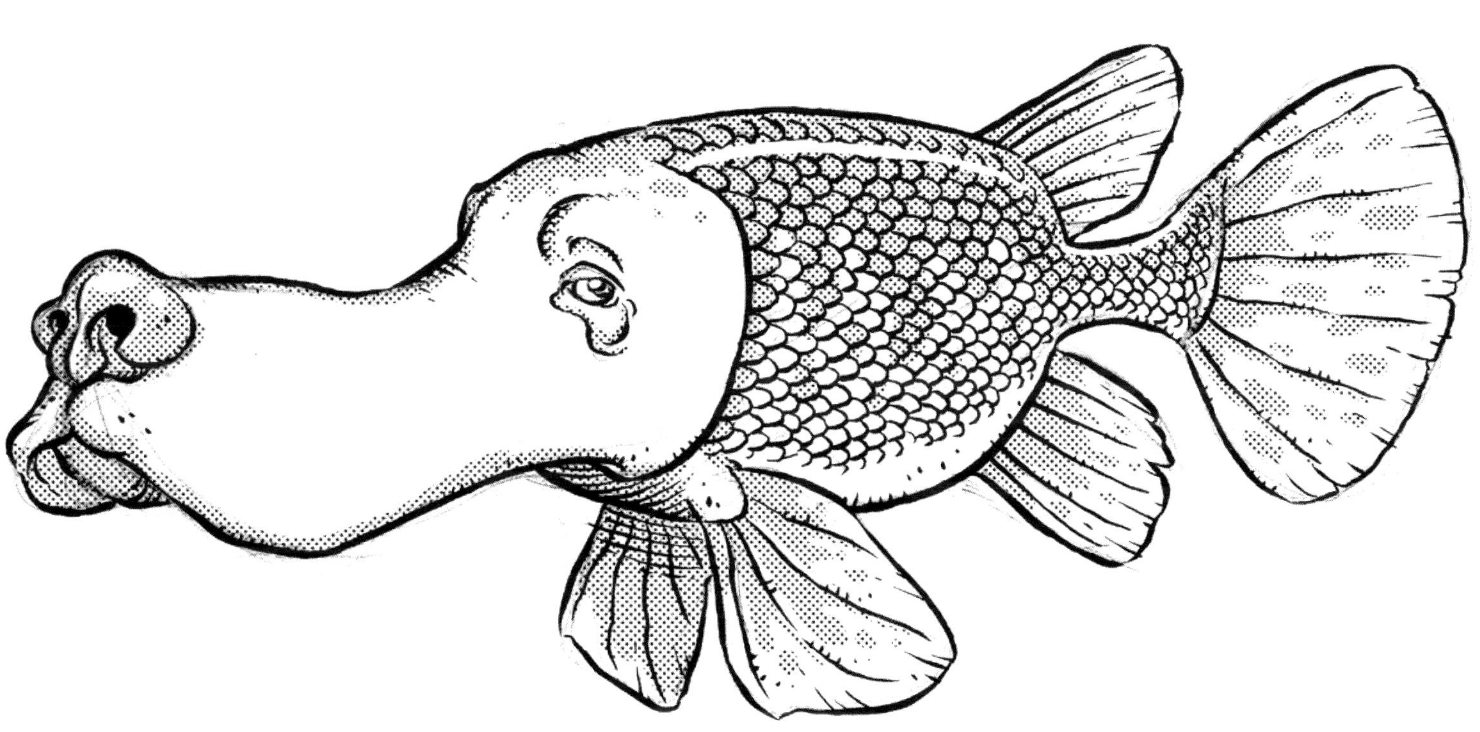

TRICERATOPS FISH

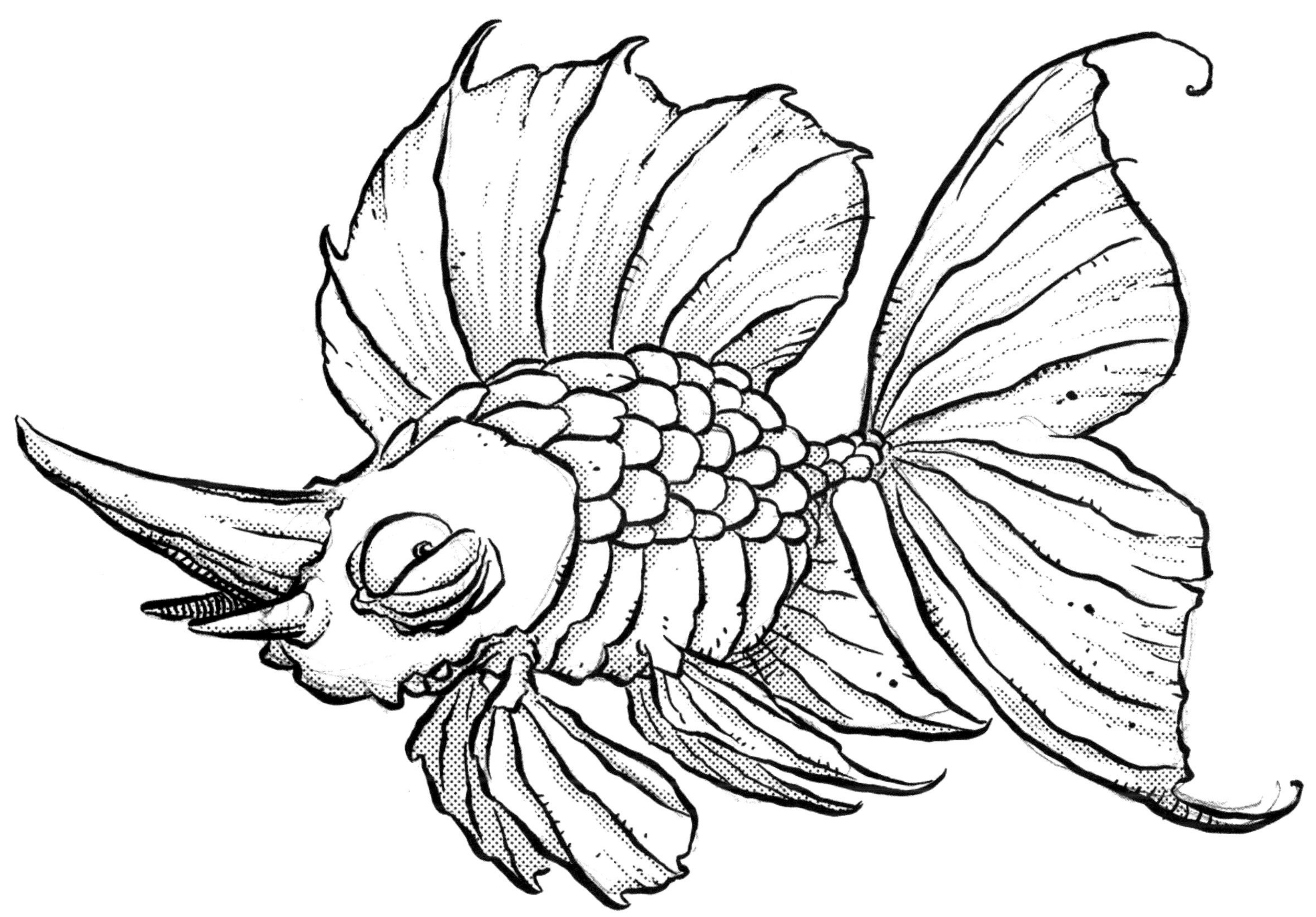

DIMETREDON FISH

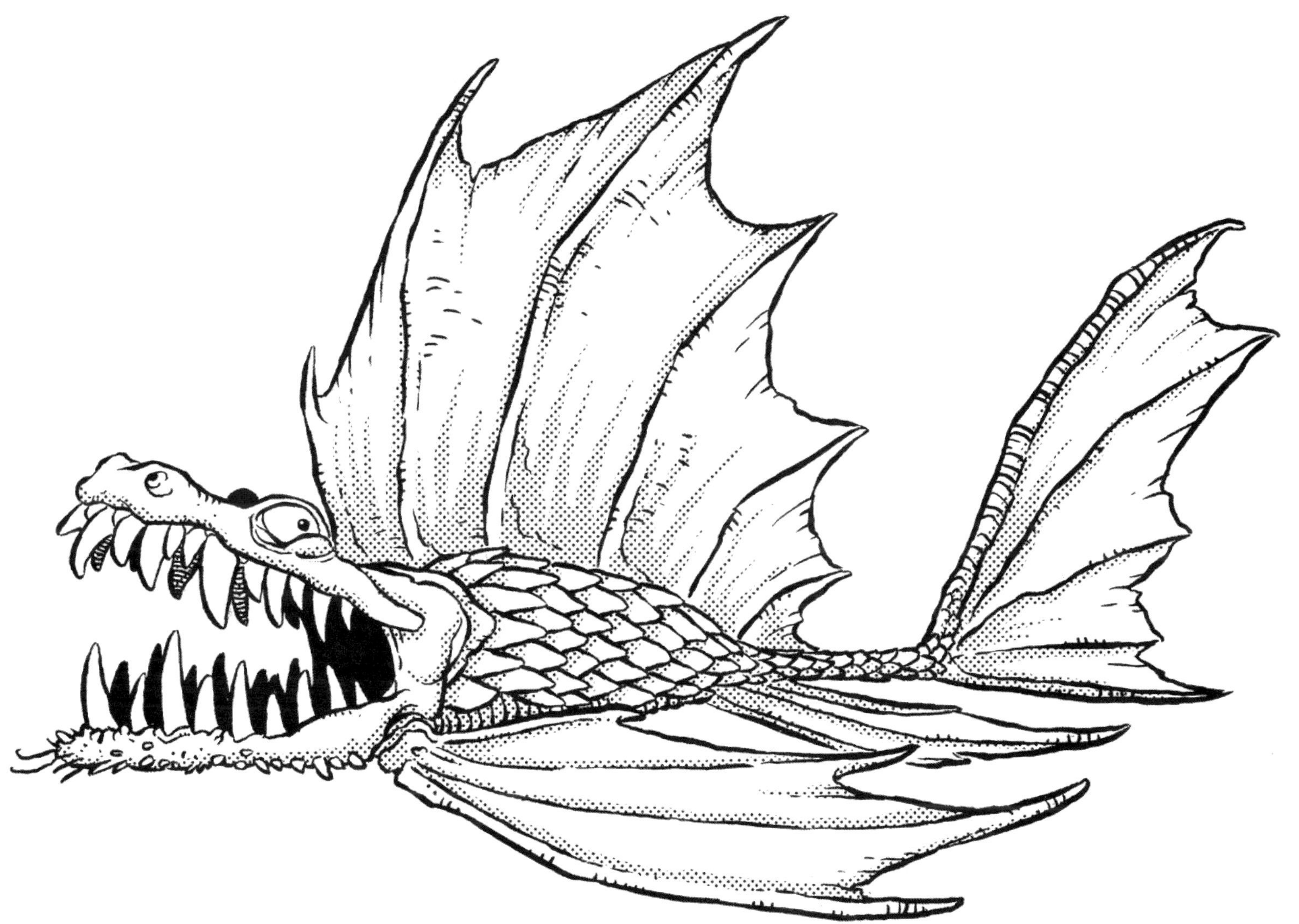

SPINY ROUNDEYE

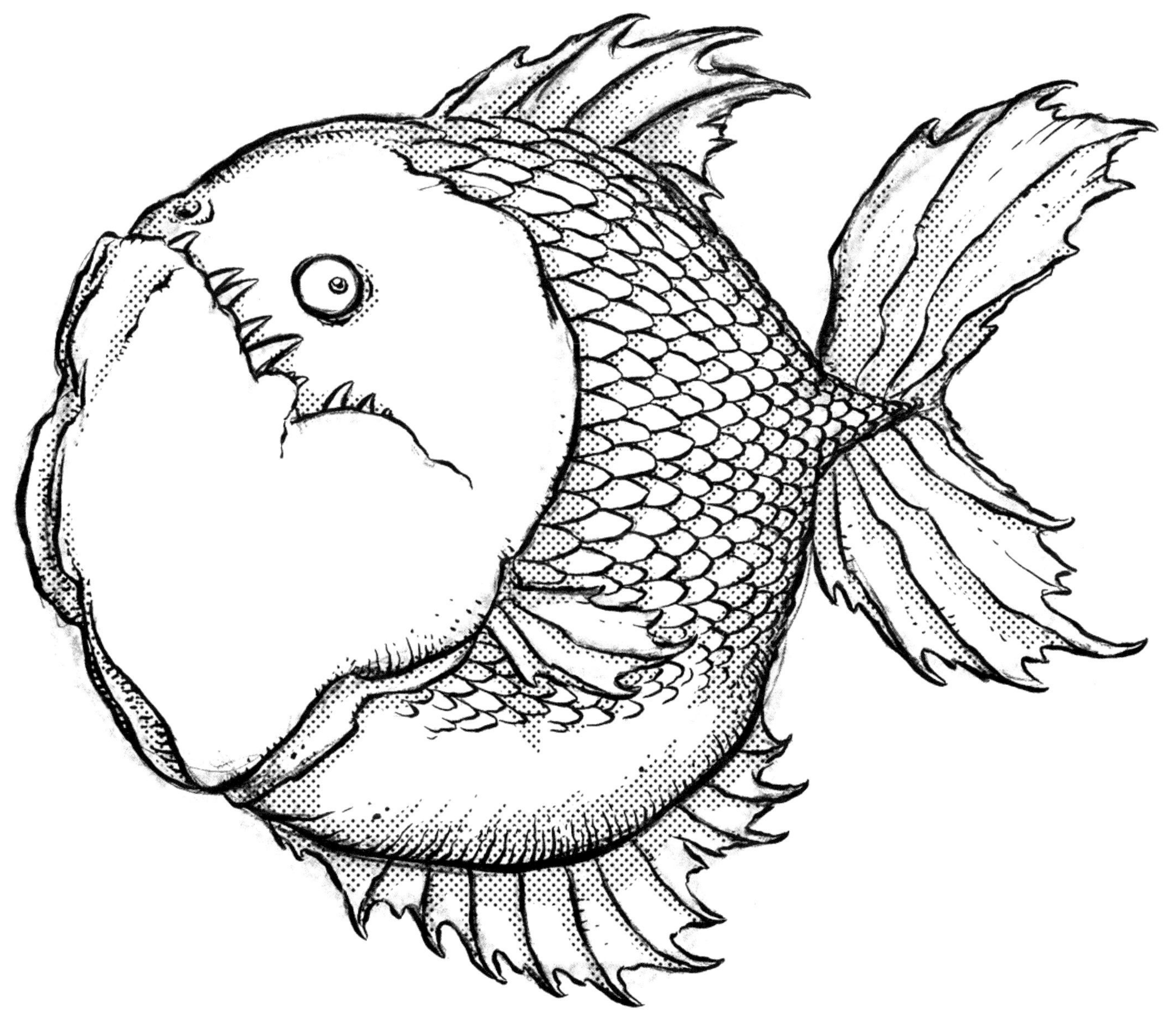

RUNT SHARK

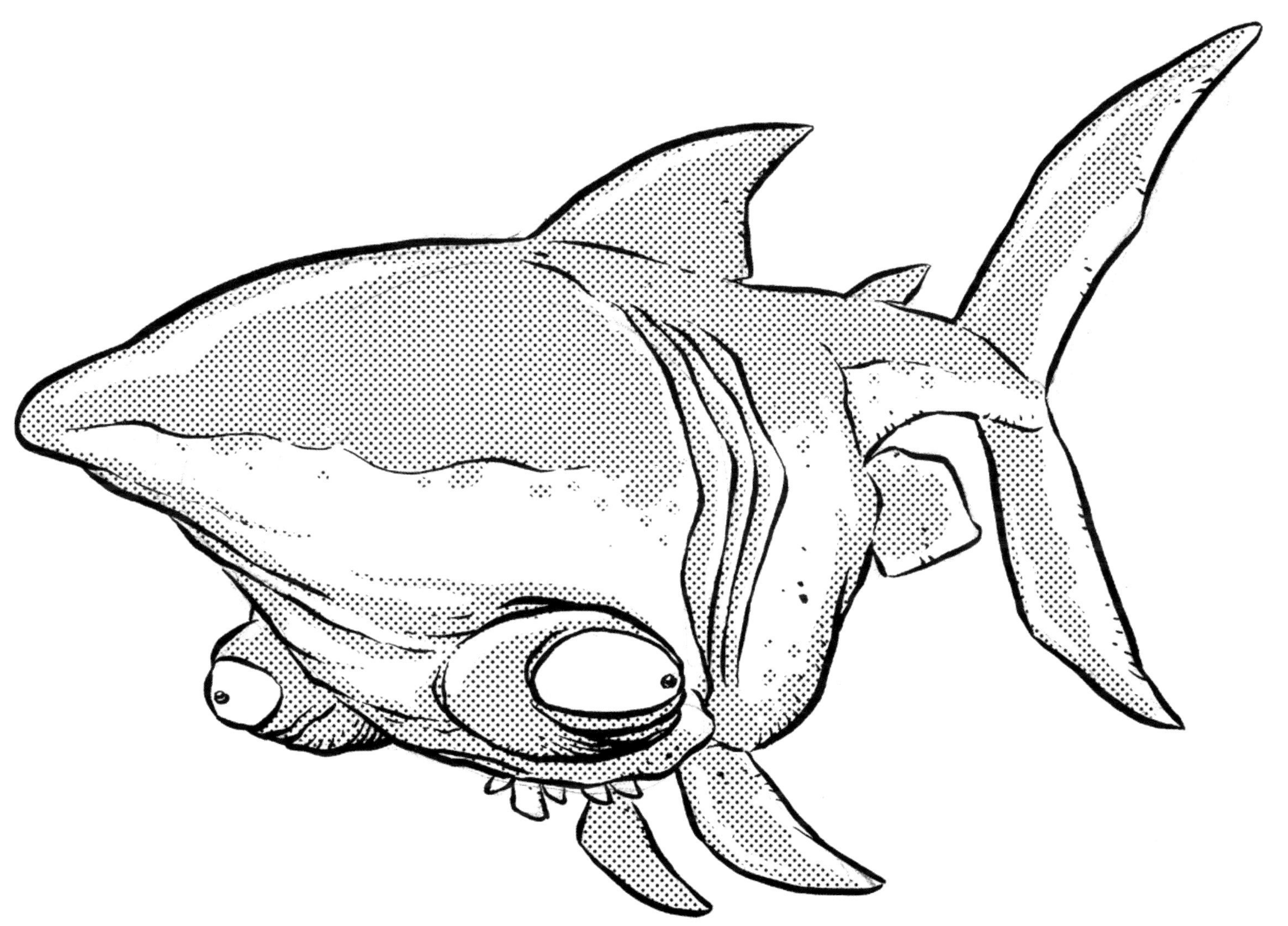

BEARDED ARMORHEAD

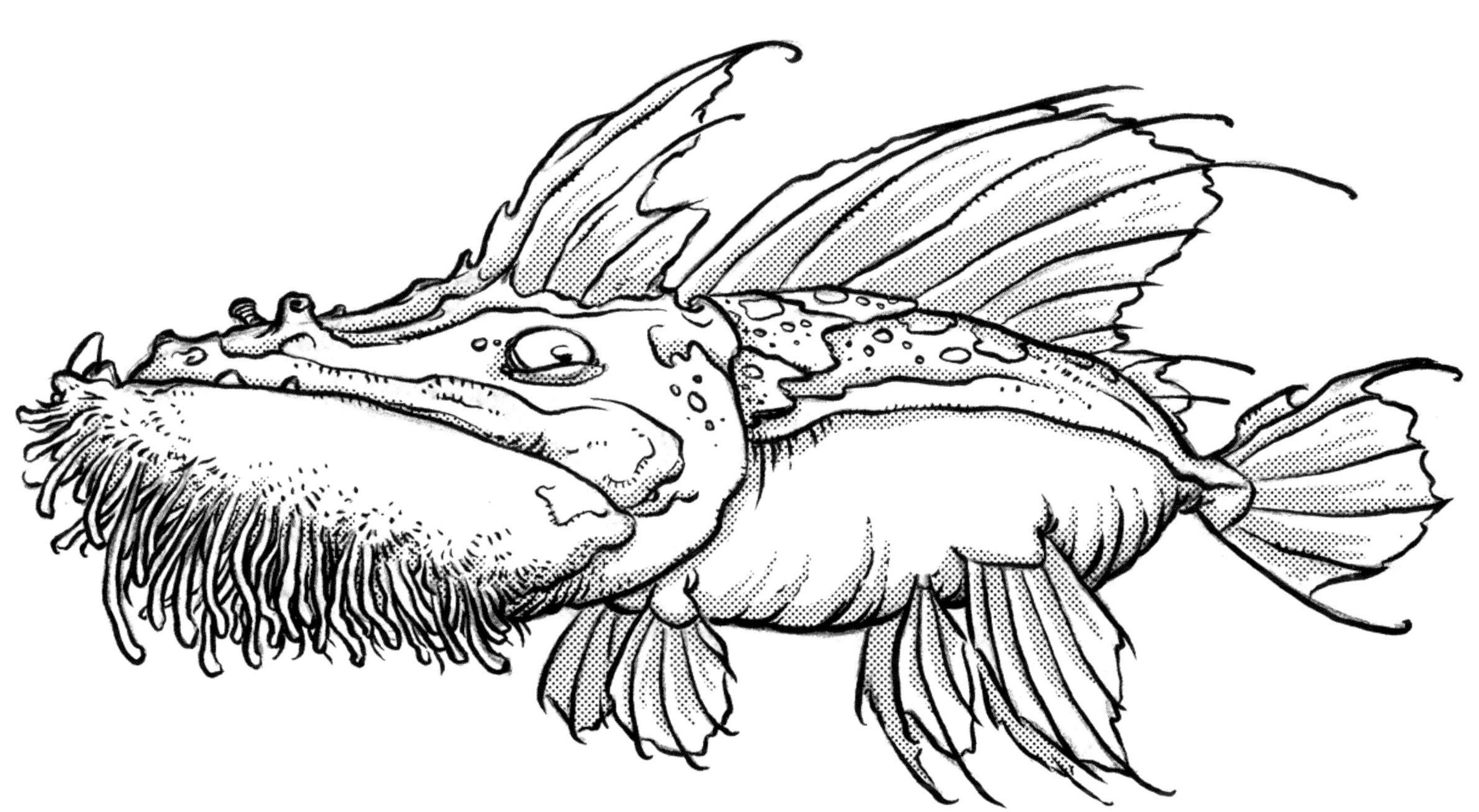

BILL NIGHY FISH

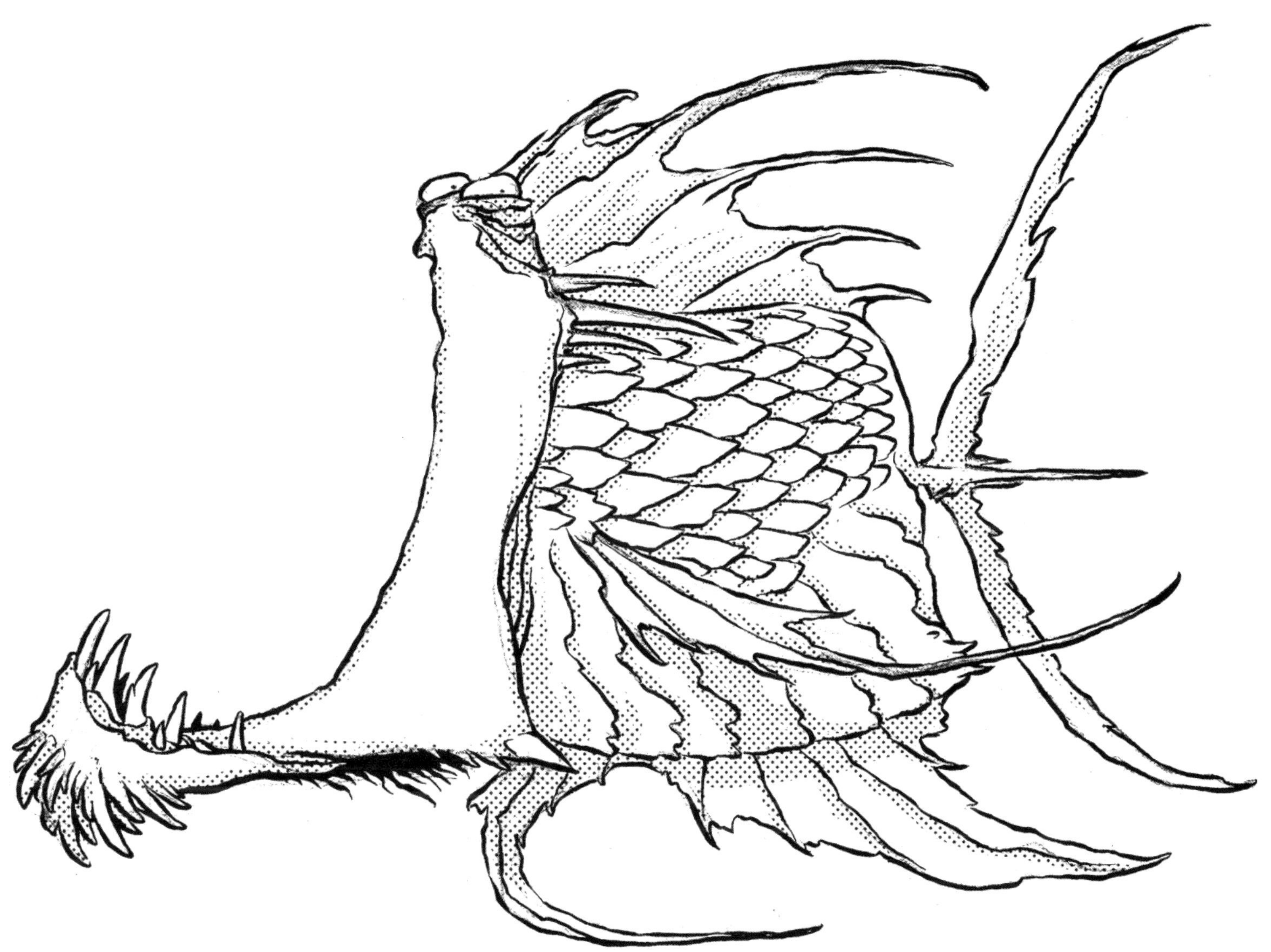

SPOTTED BELLY RAILFISH

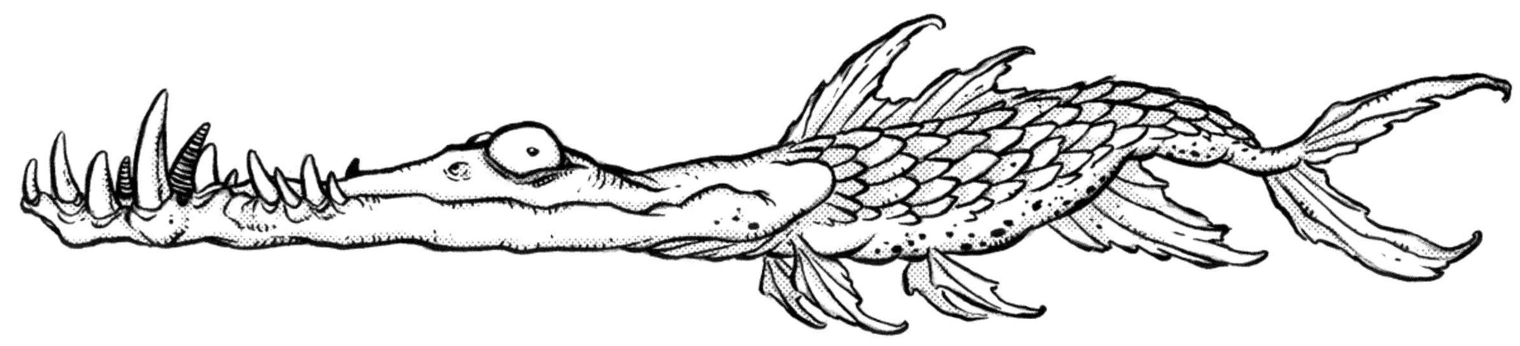

HORNED FLATFACE

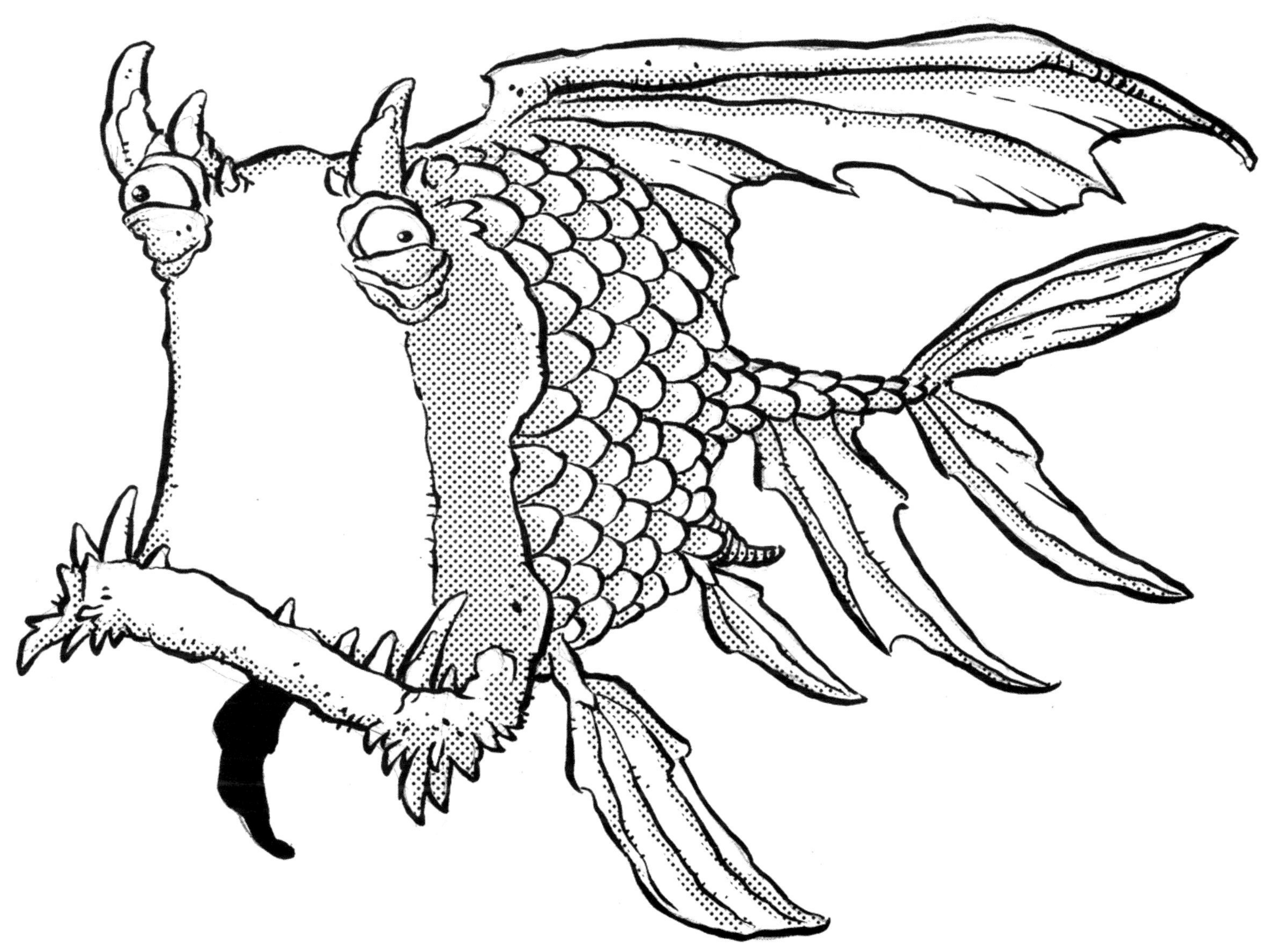

BLOATED FRECKLEFACE

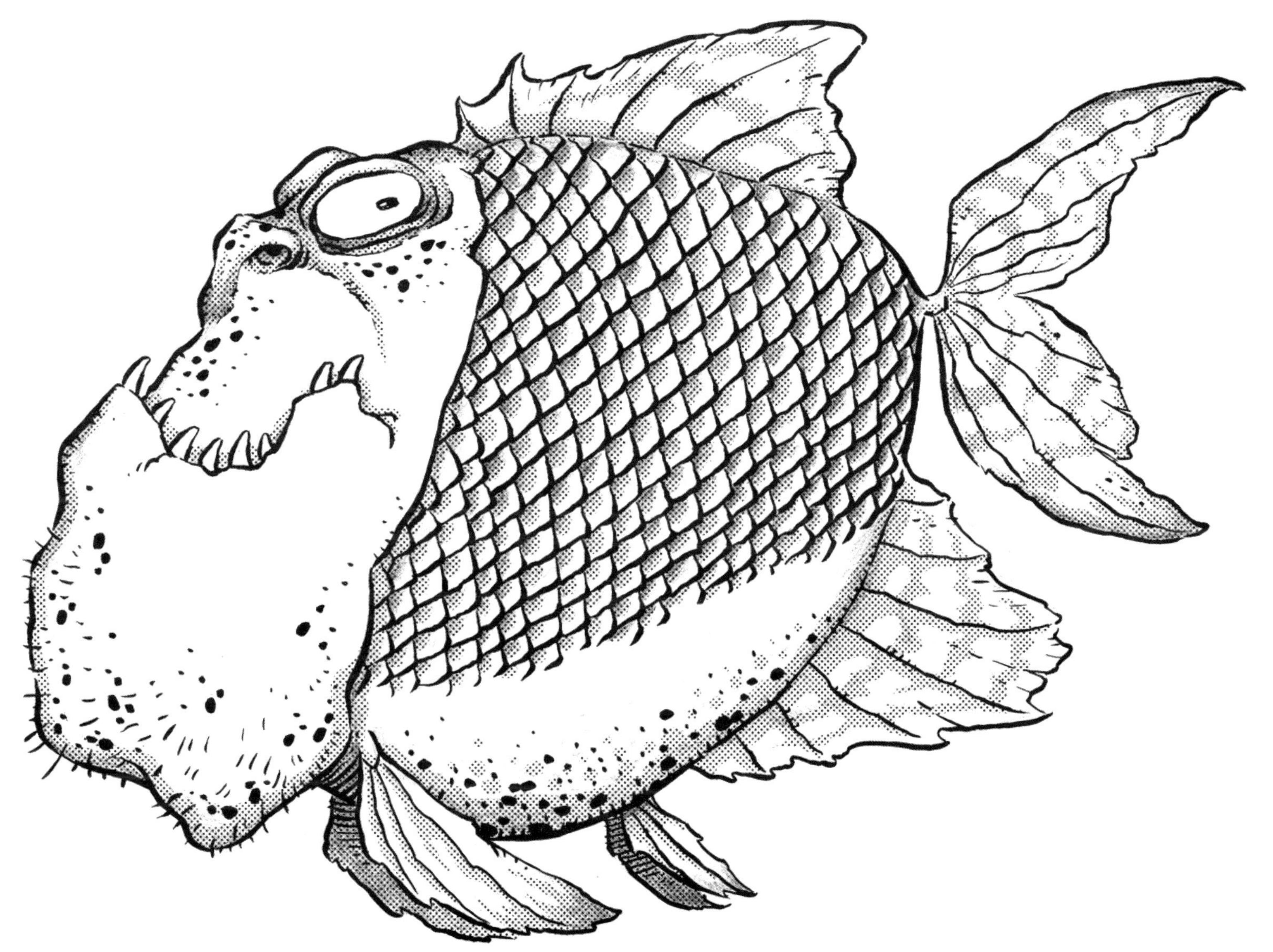

TOOTHY SPEEDFIN

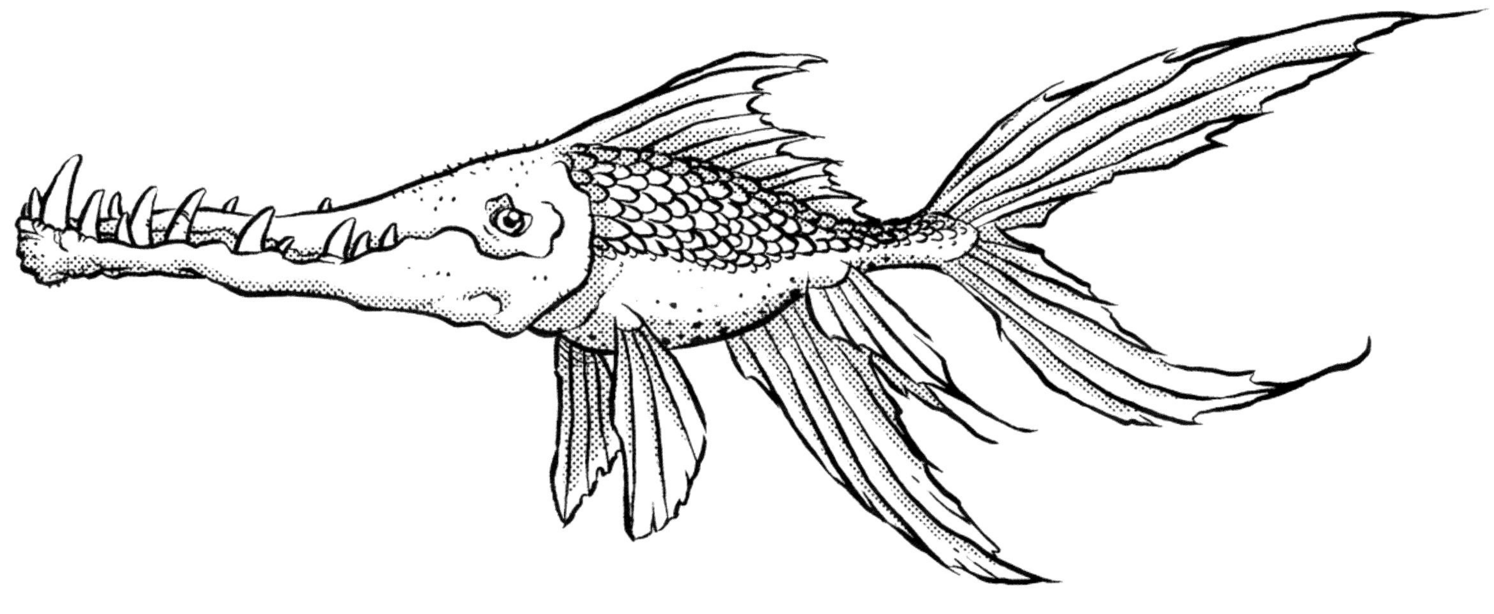

LONG-SNOUTED CREEPYFIN

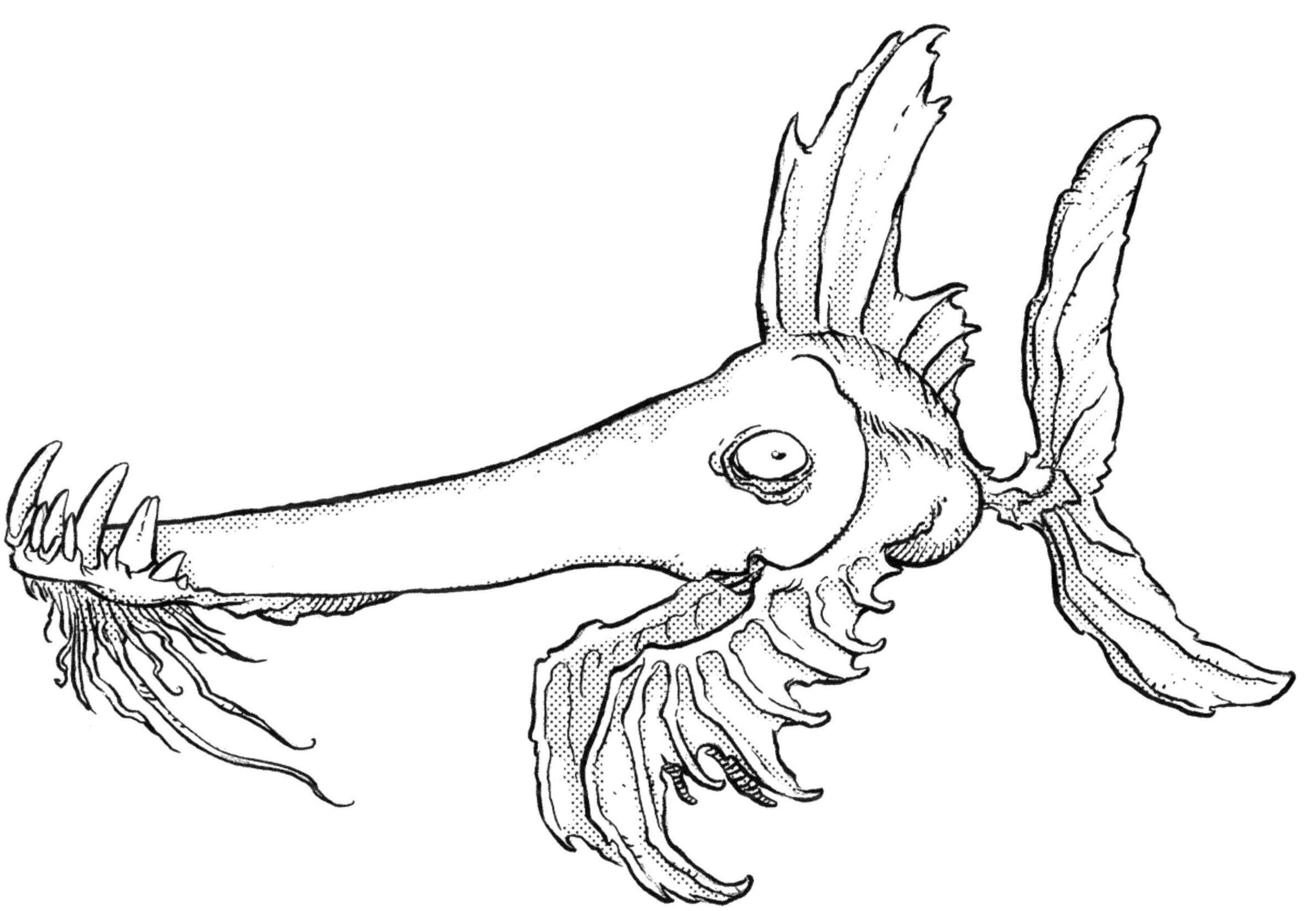

POMPADOUR FISH

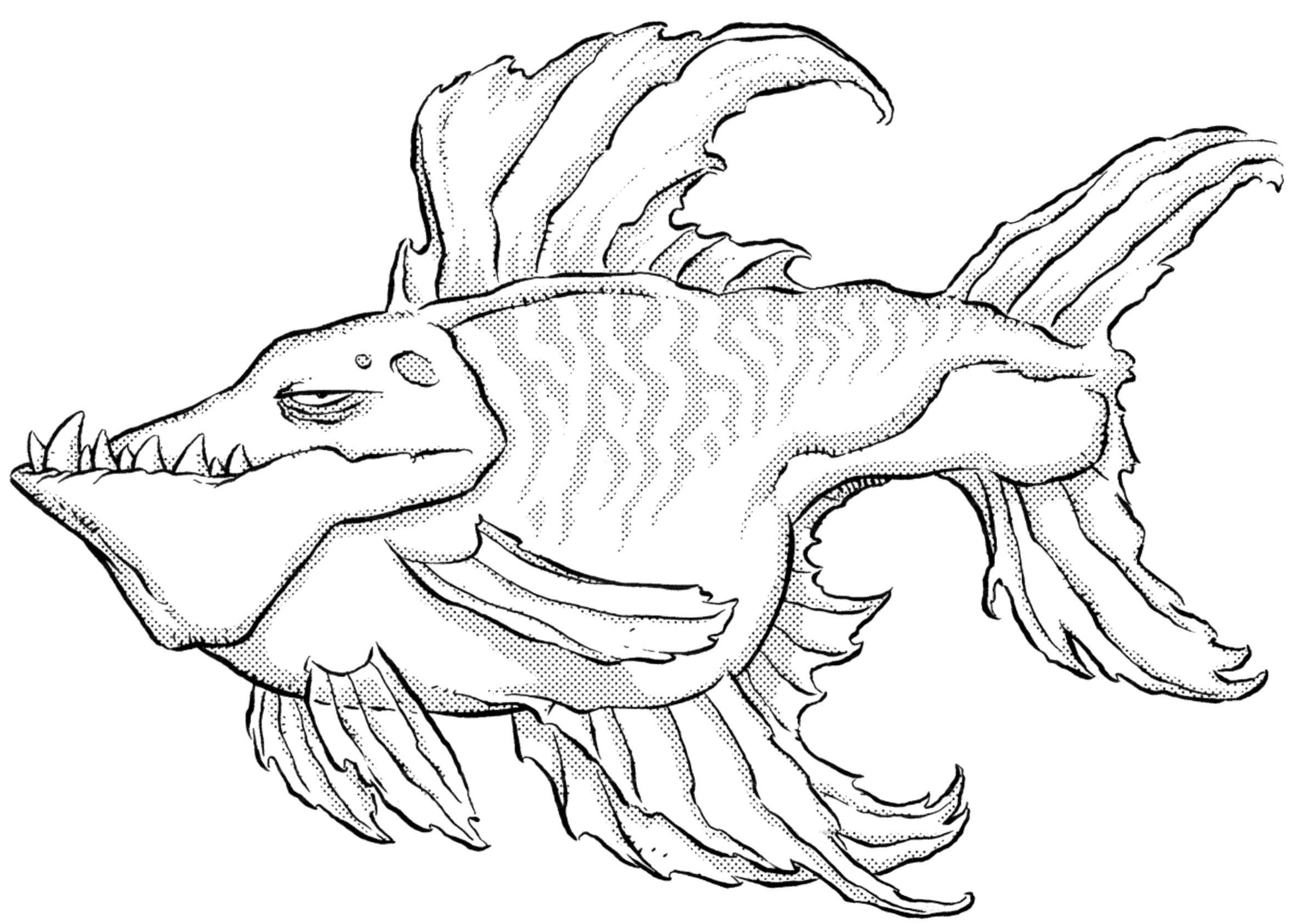

SPINDLE FIN

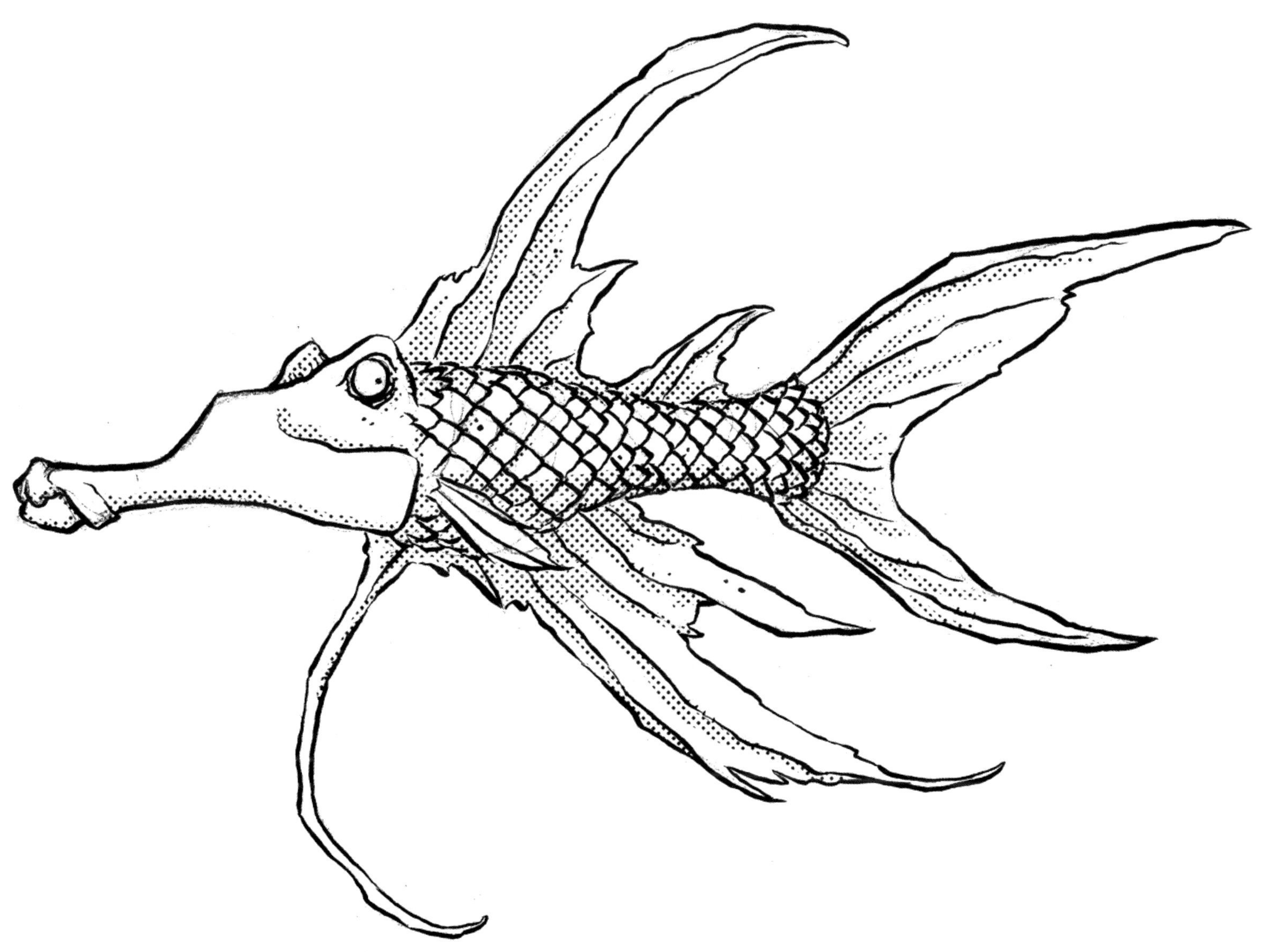

BLUE-BELLIED WORMNECK

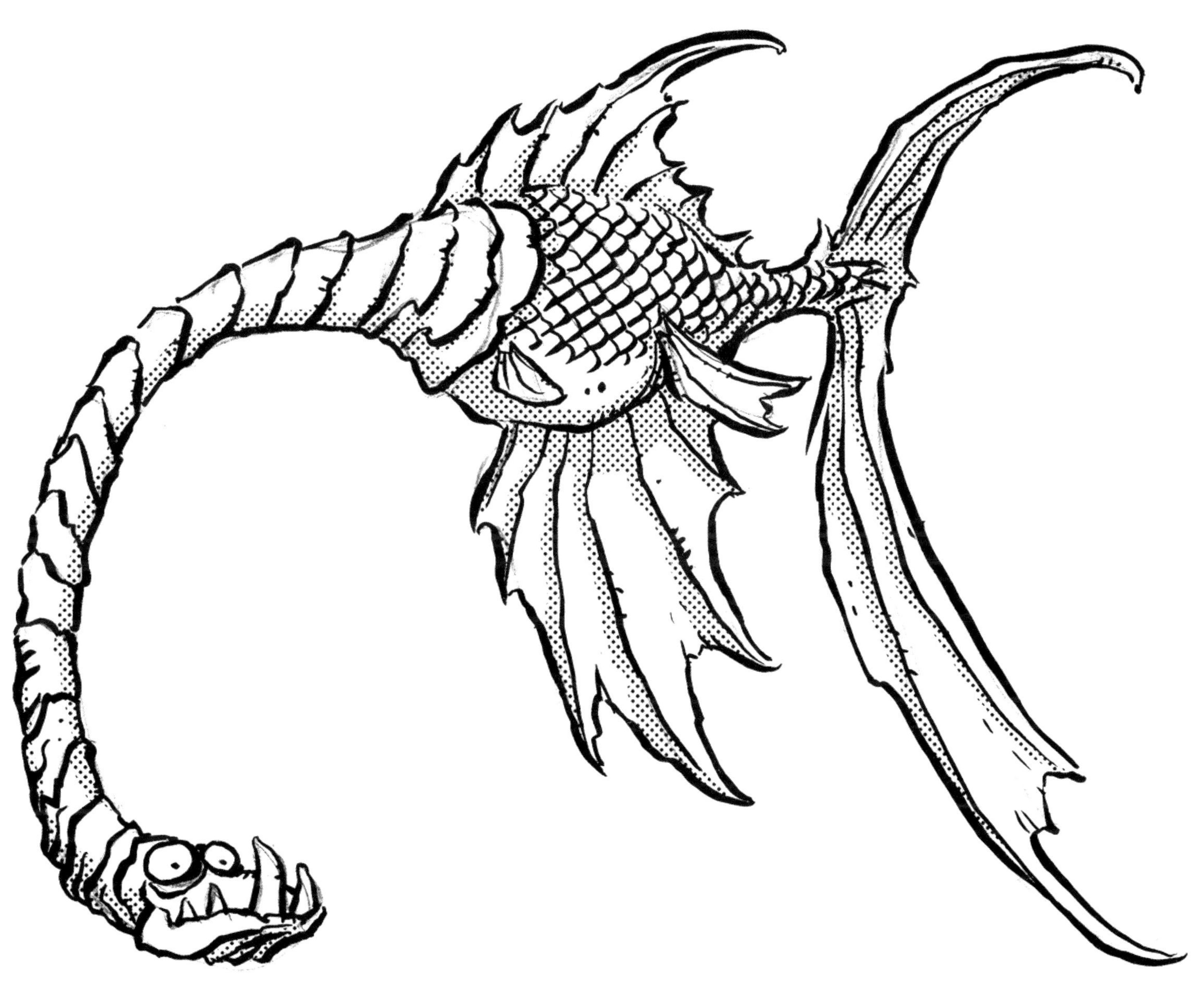

BIG LIP BASS

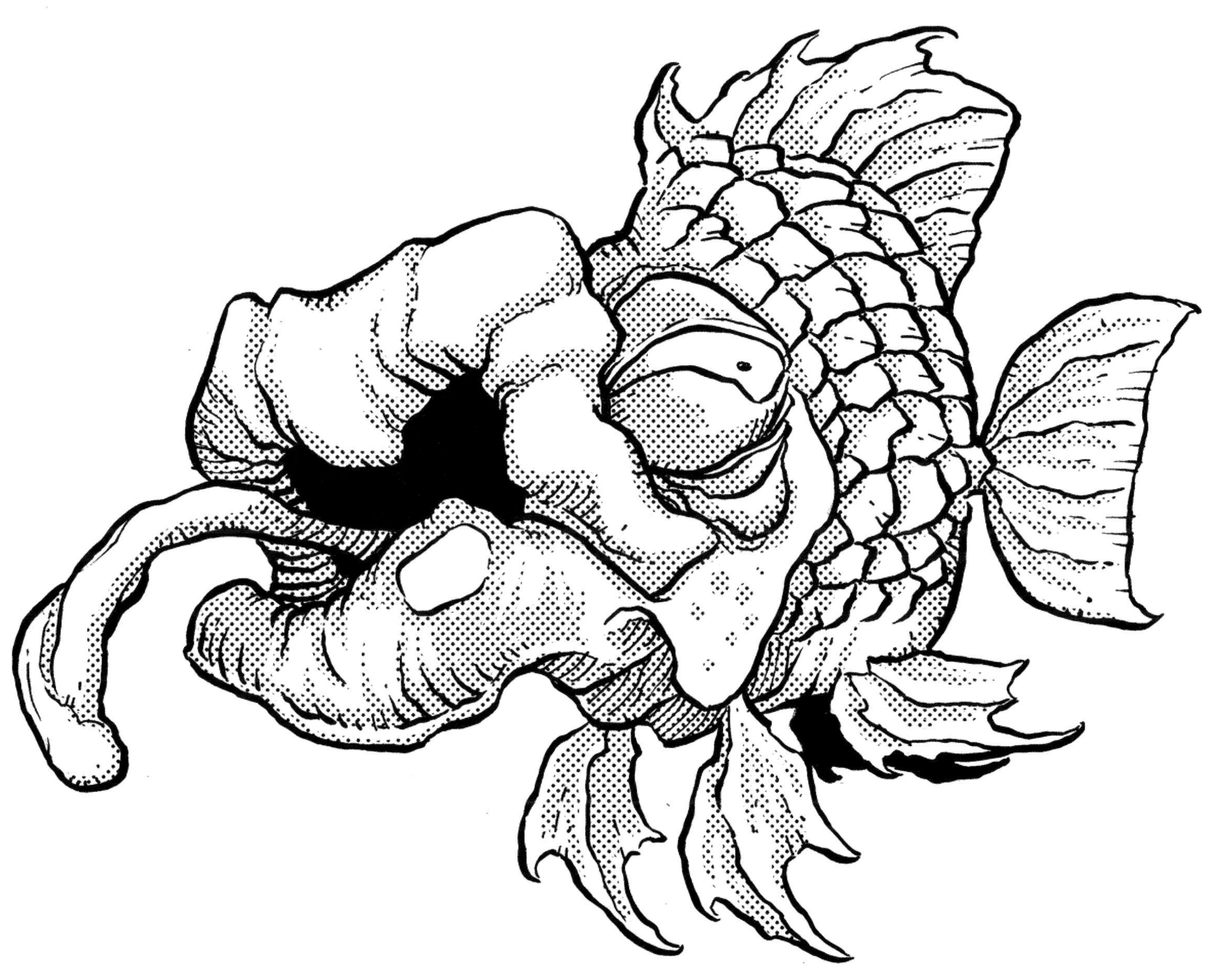

COTTAGE FISH

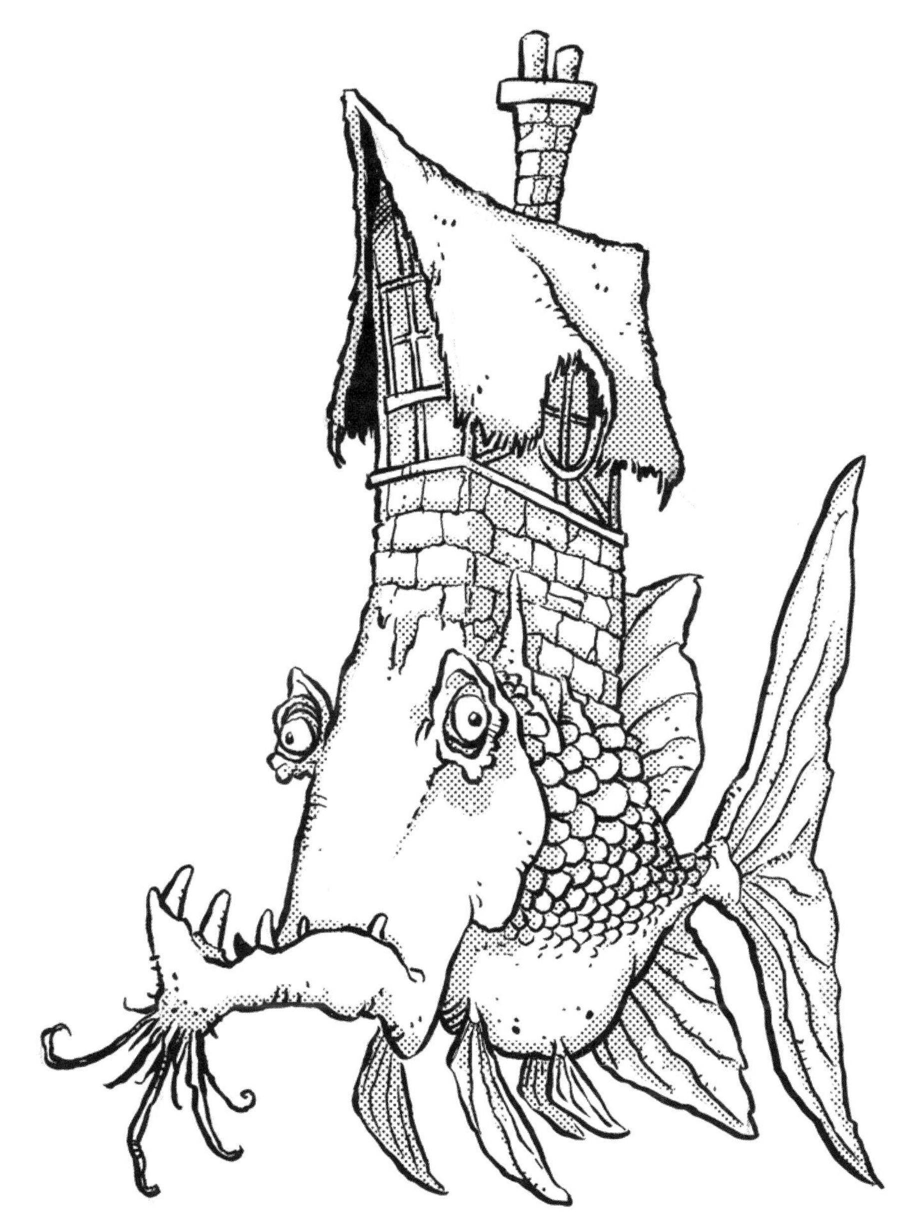

CLEVER FISH

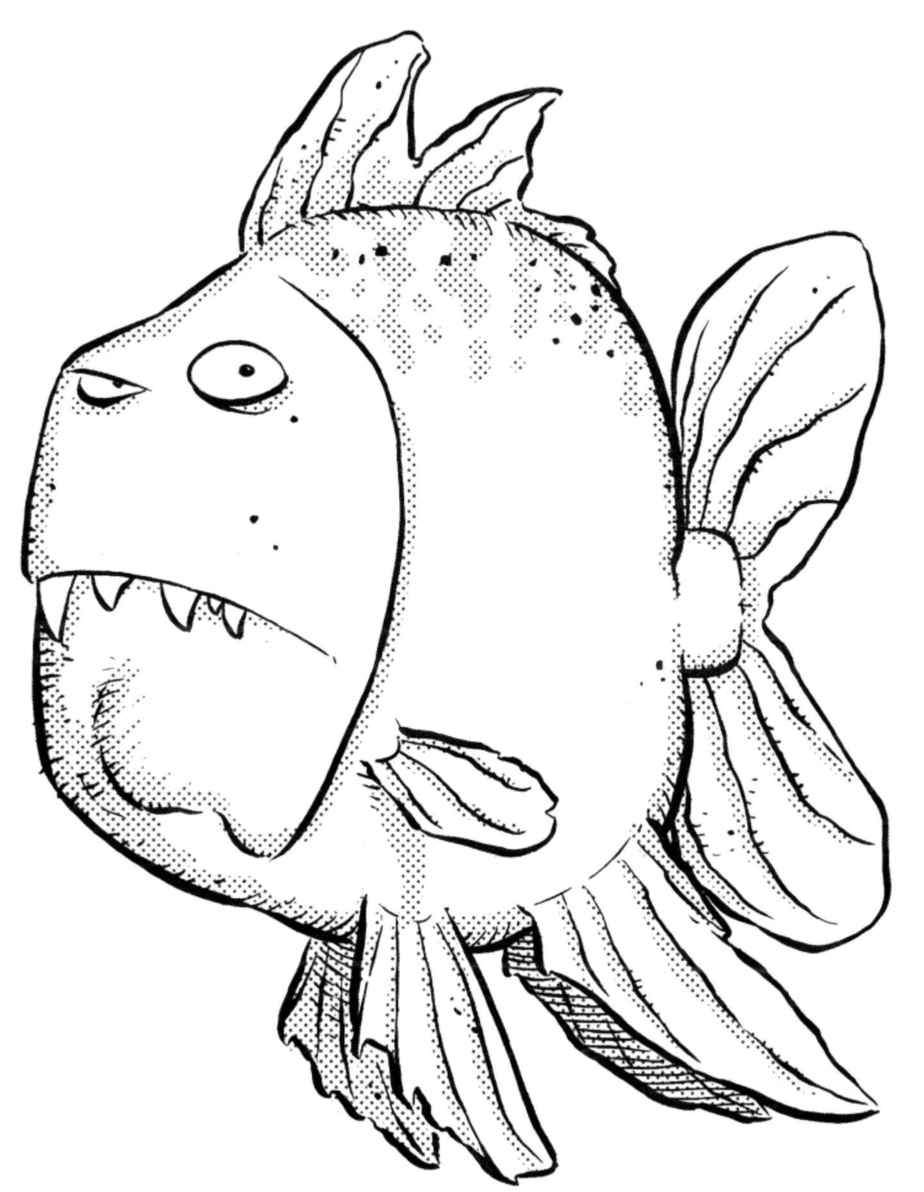

STRIPED DUCKFACE

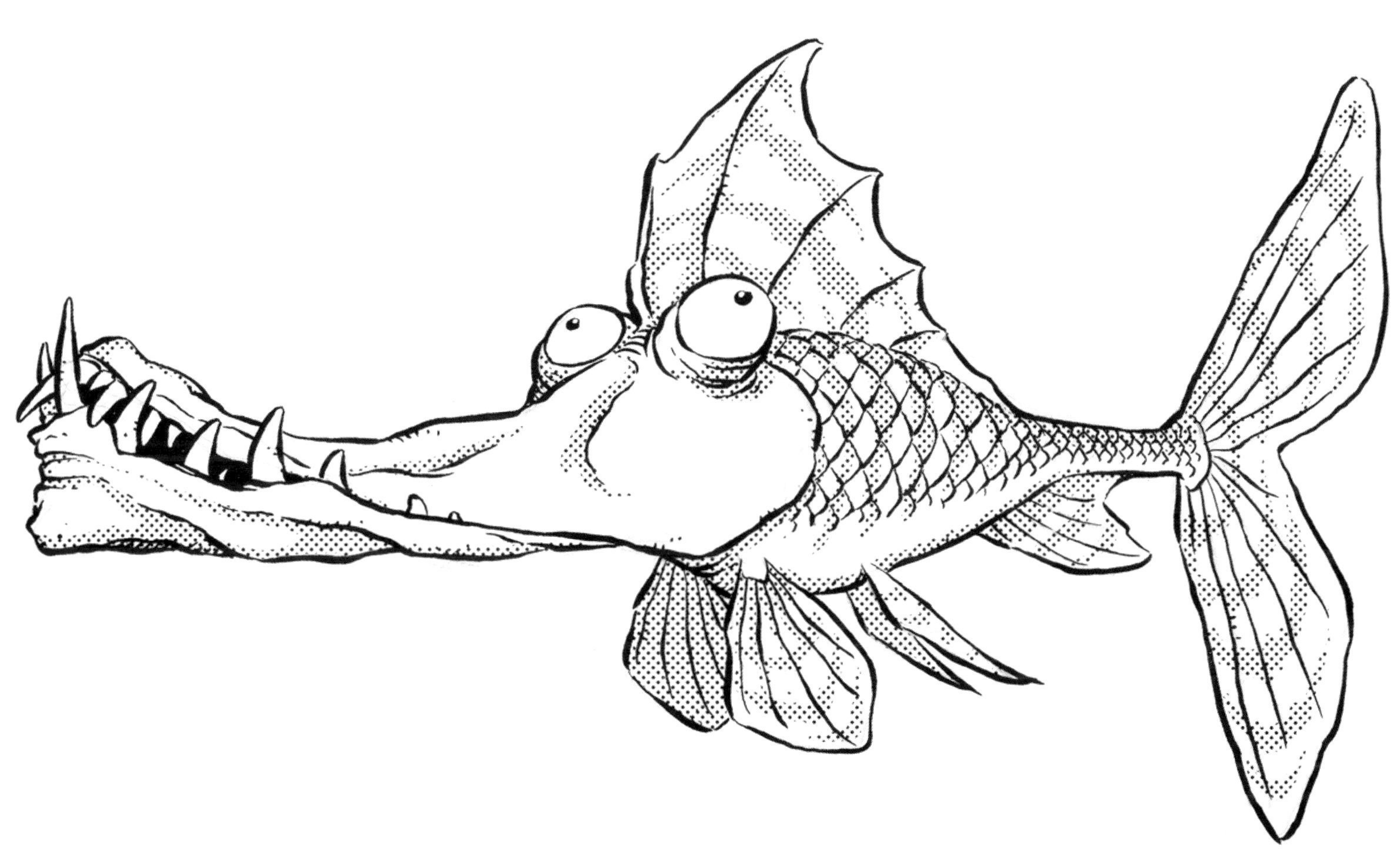

SALTON SINK TRICERATROUT

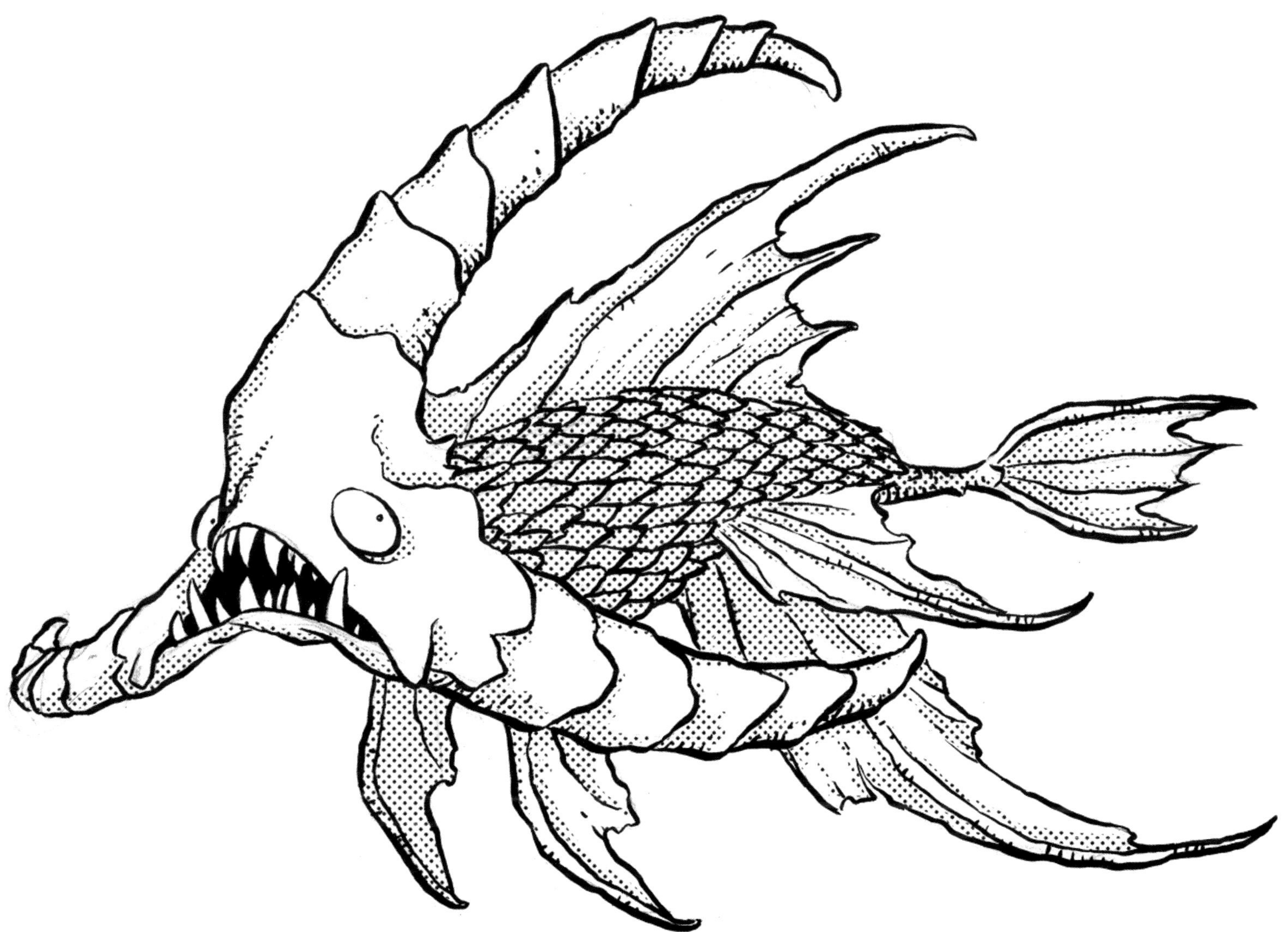

ERNEST THE RIDGE-BACKED SNAIL EYE

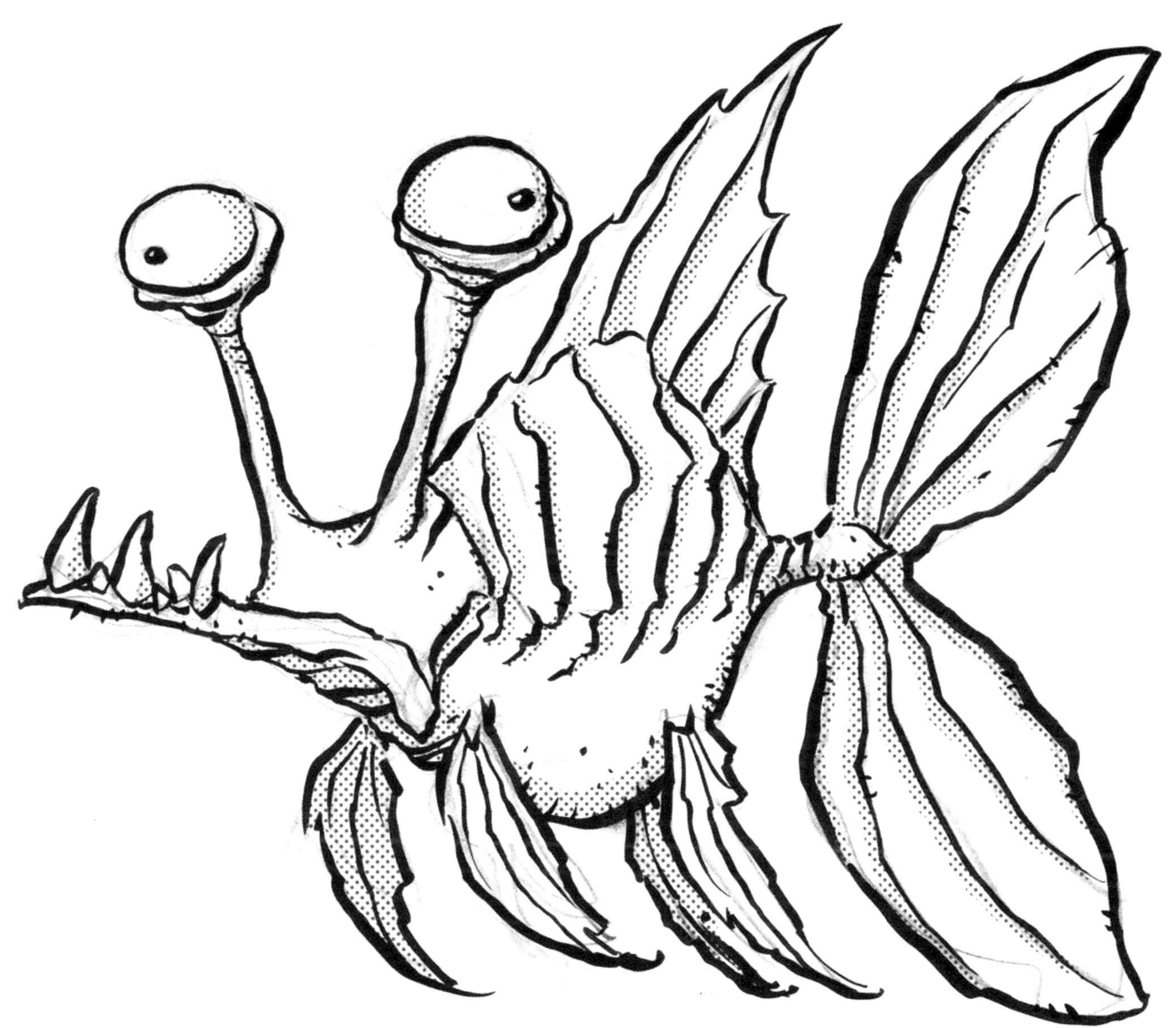

LONG-WHISKERED DRAGONHEAD

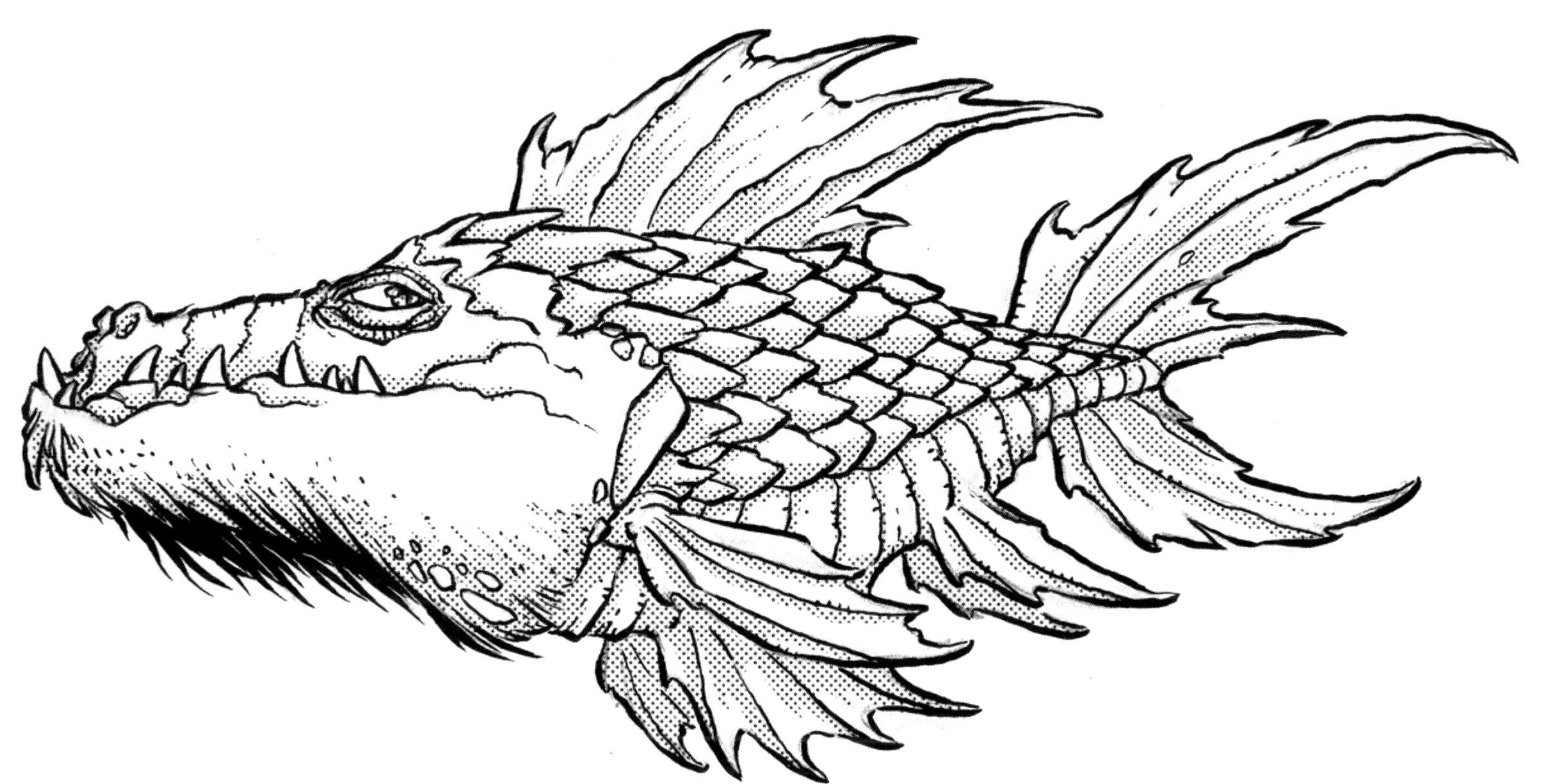

ME-BEFORE-BRACES FISH

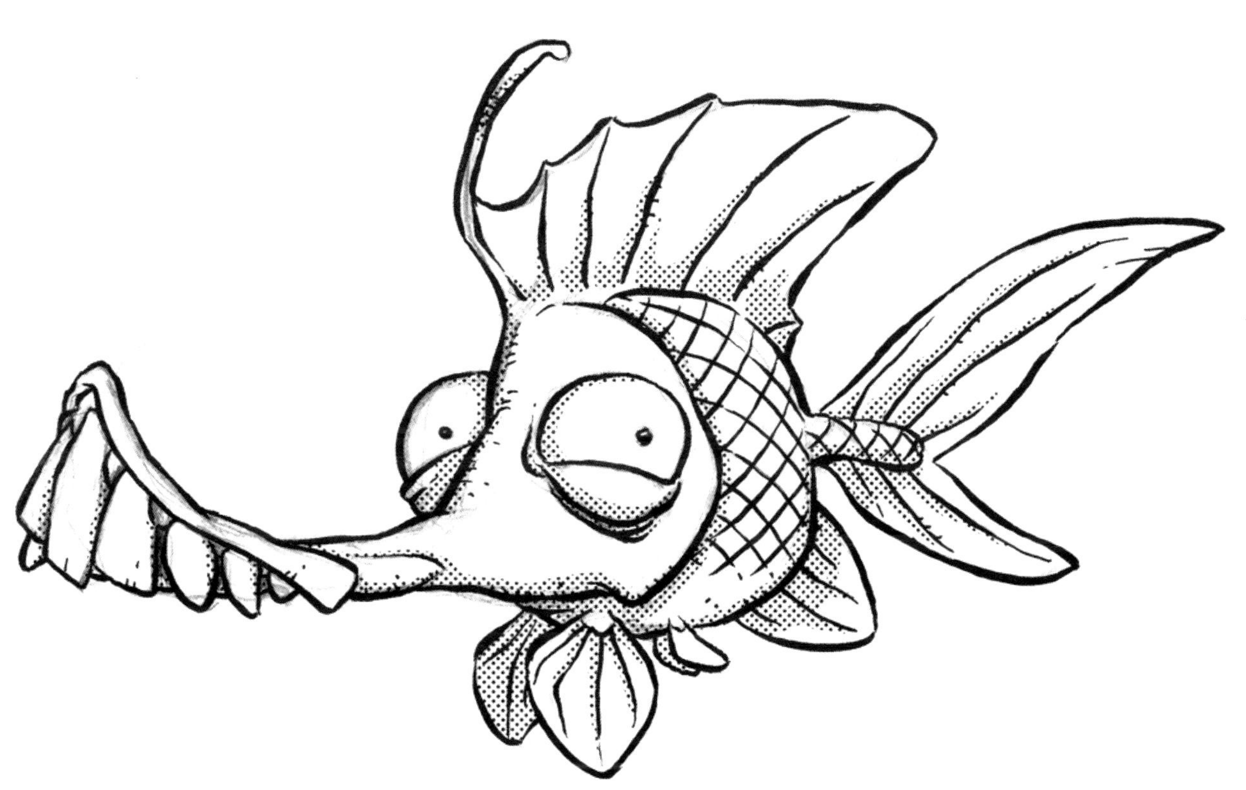

BULL-HEADED MOSSJAW

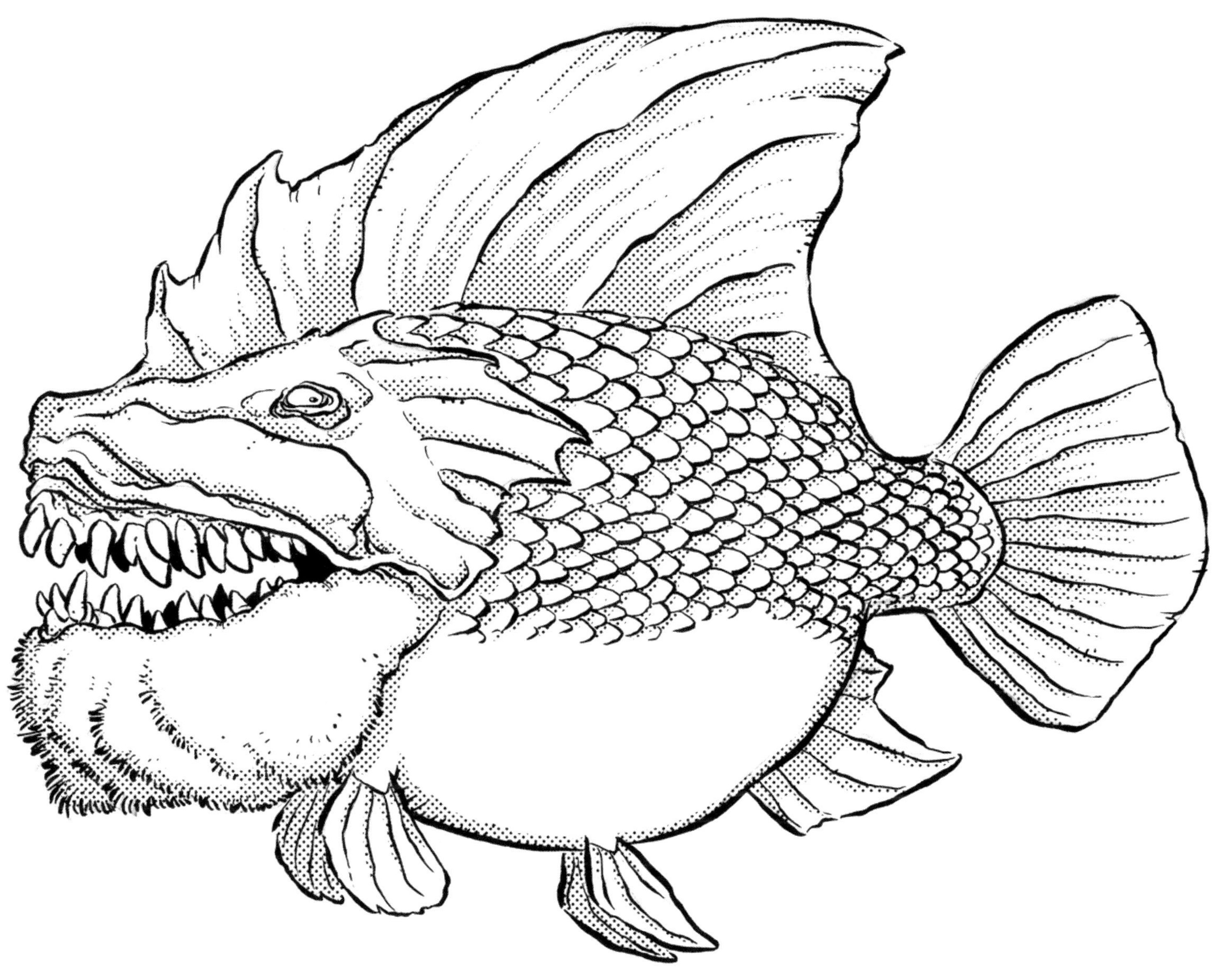

LACE FISH

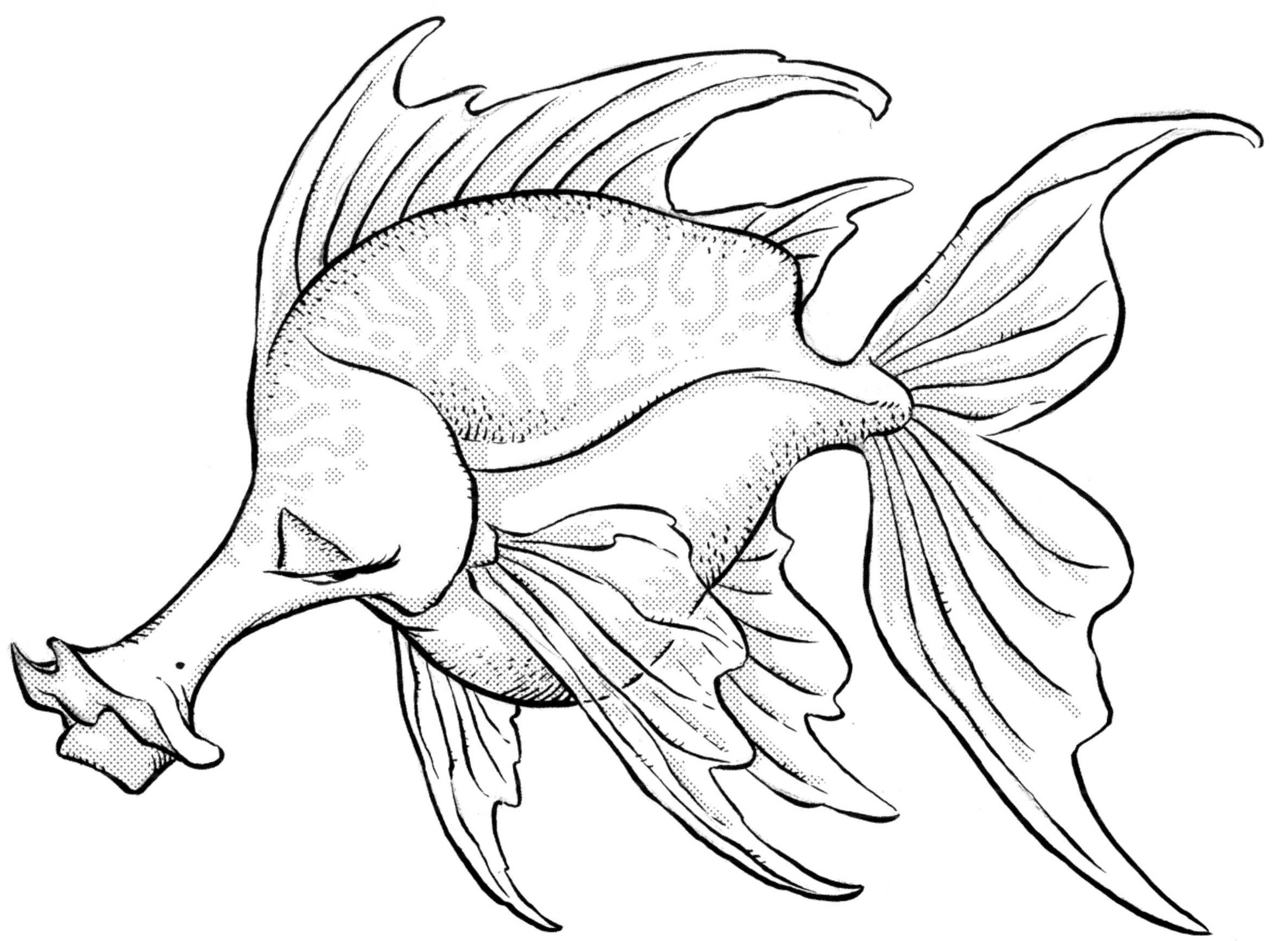

LONG-SNOUTED FIREFIN

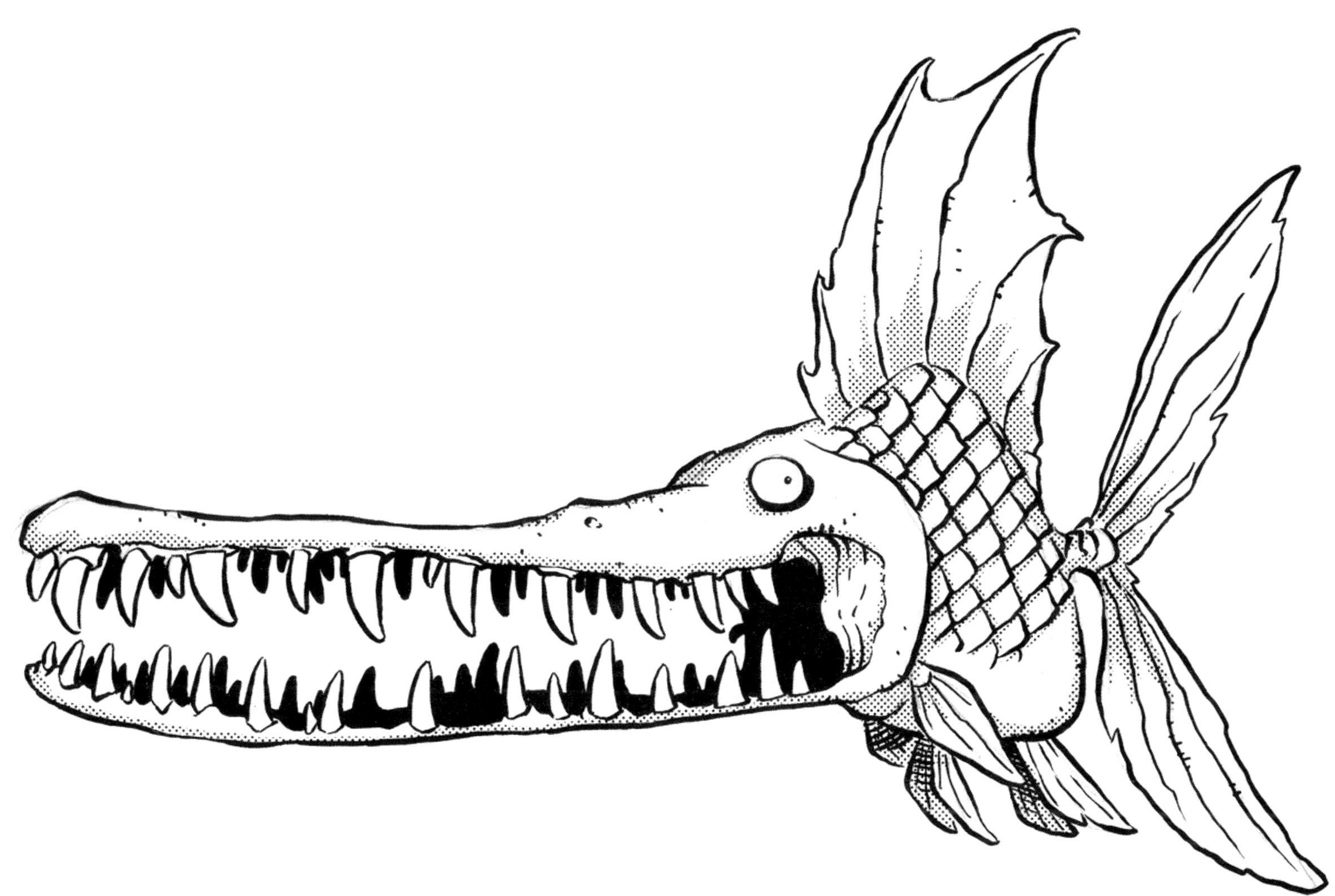

FRILLED SHARKHEAD

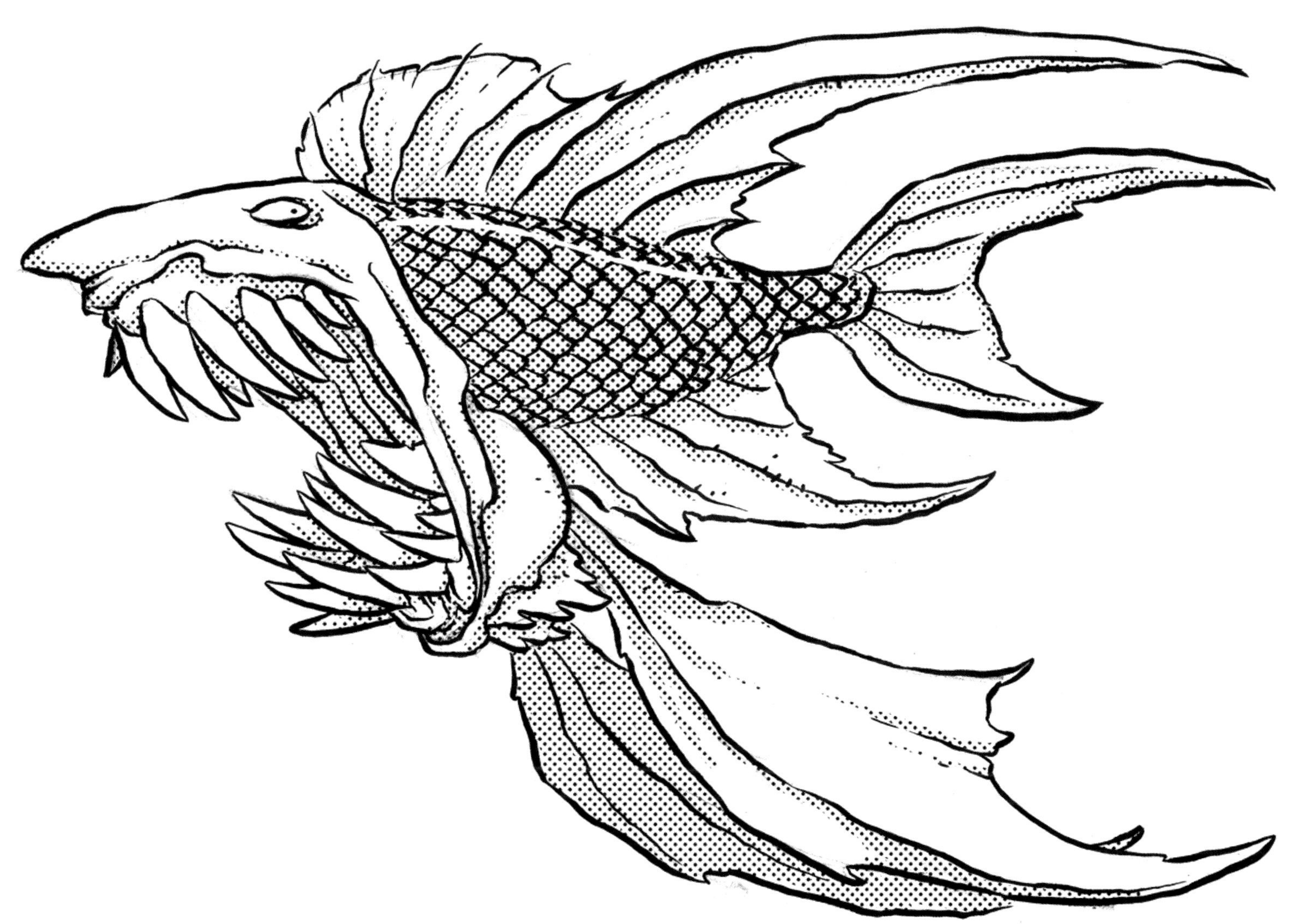

BEARDED GOOGLEFISH

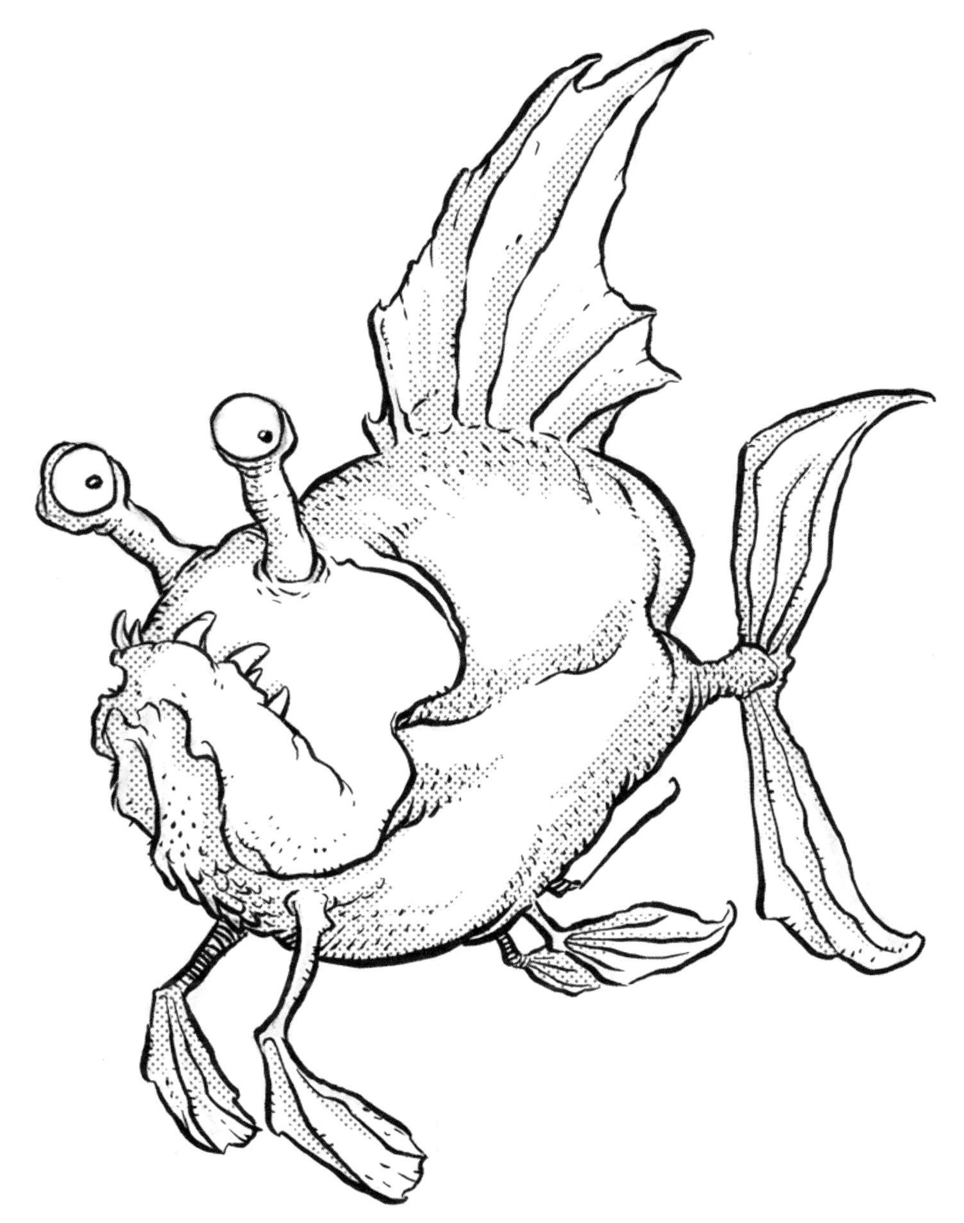

ANTENNA LONG WHISKER

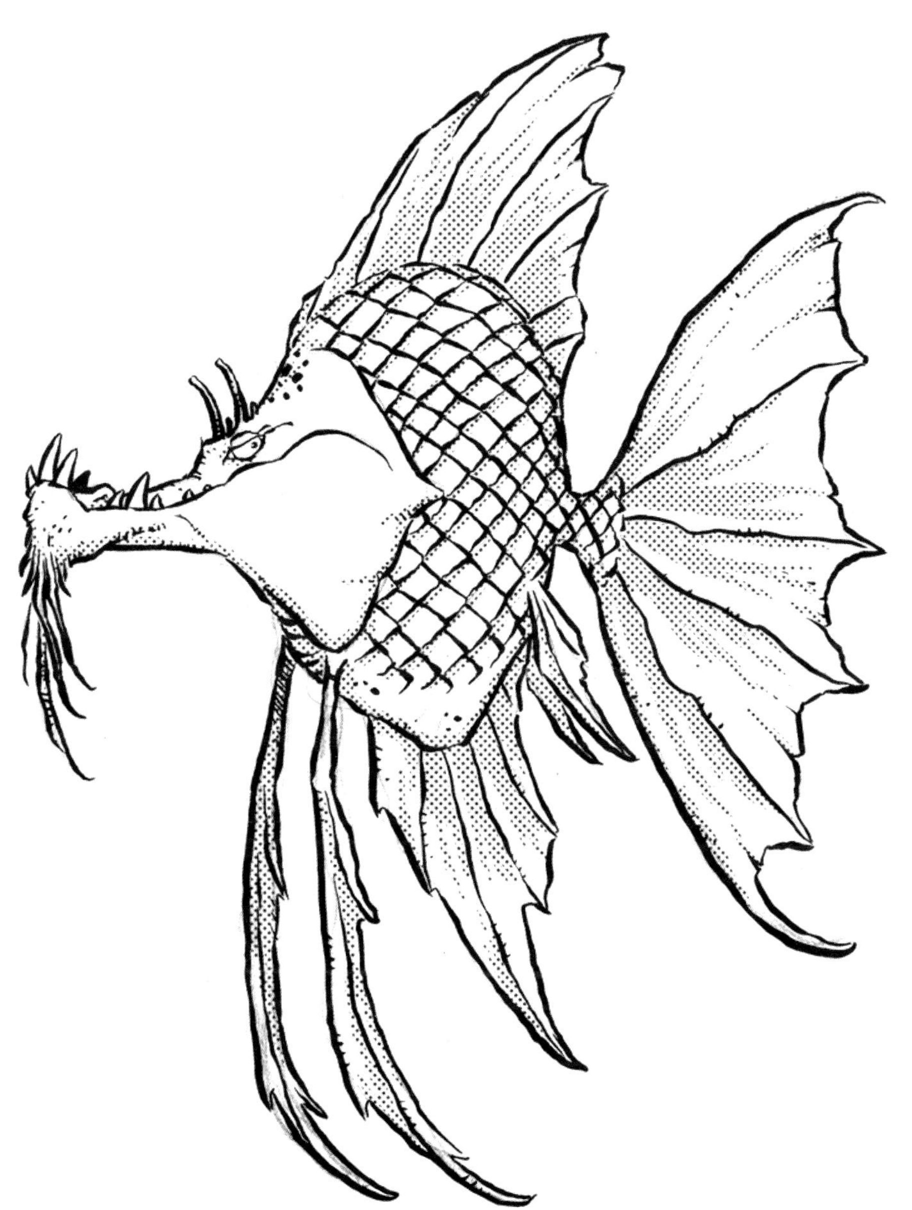

GRUMPY FATBELLY

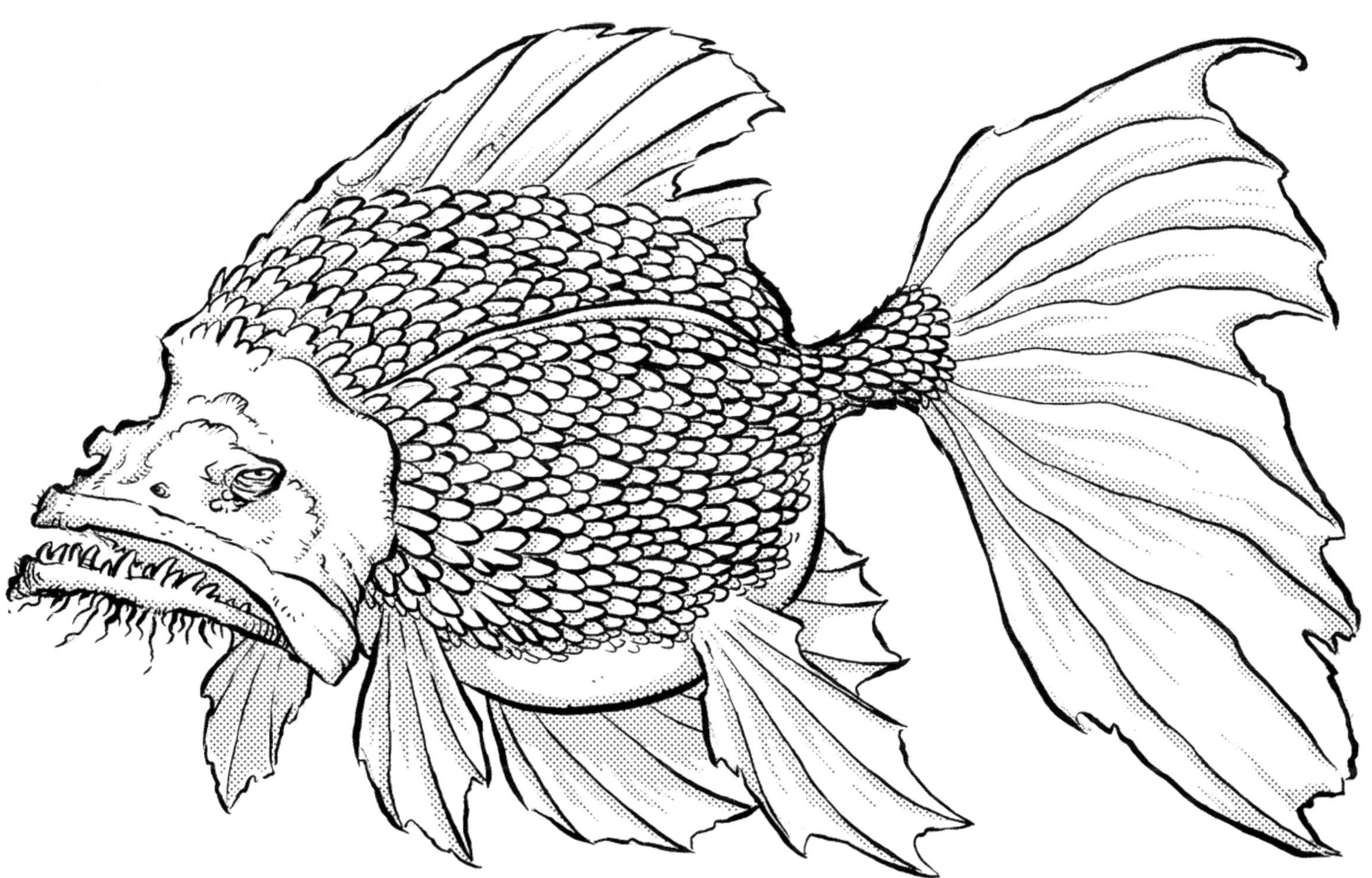

GREEN-BELLIED SPOONFISH

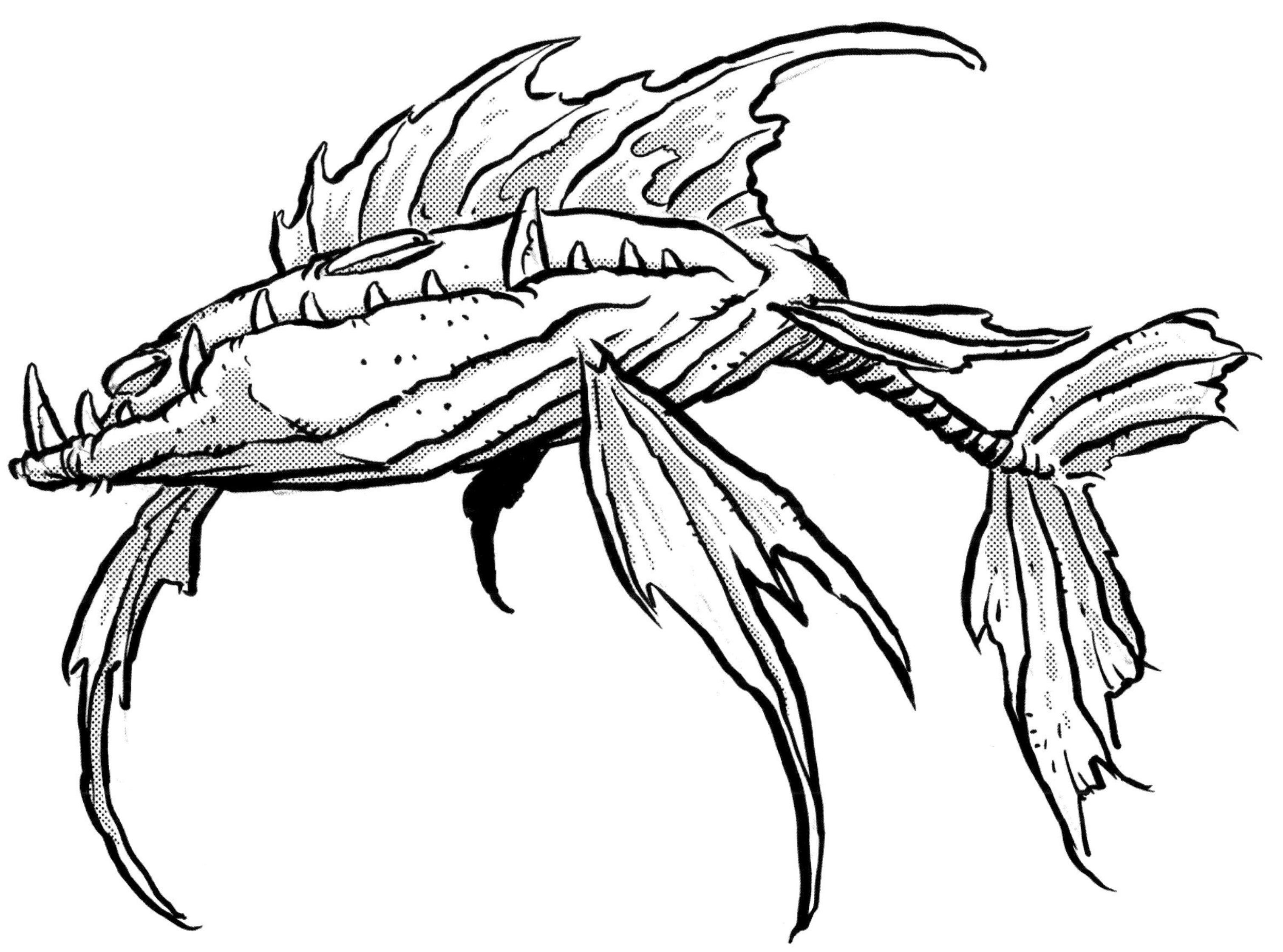

SNOZ FISH

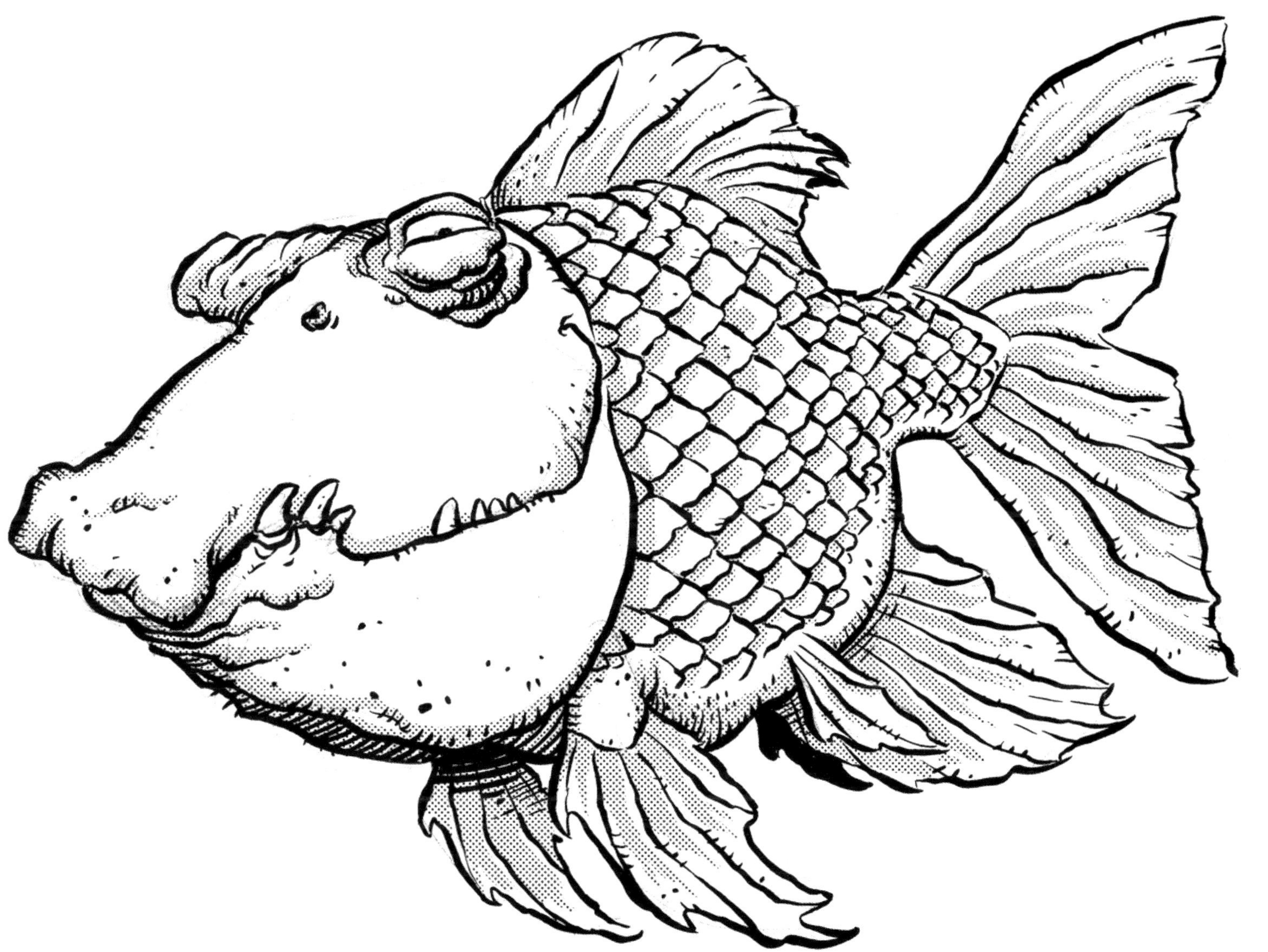

SPOTTED SNOUT FISH

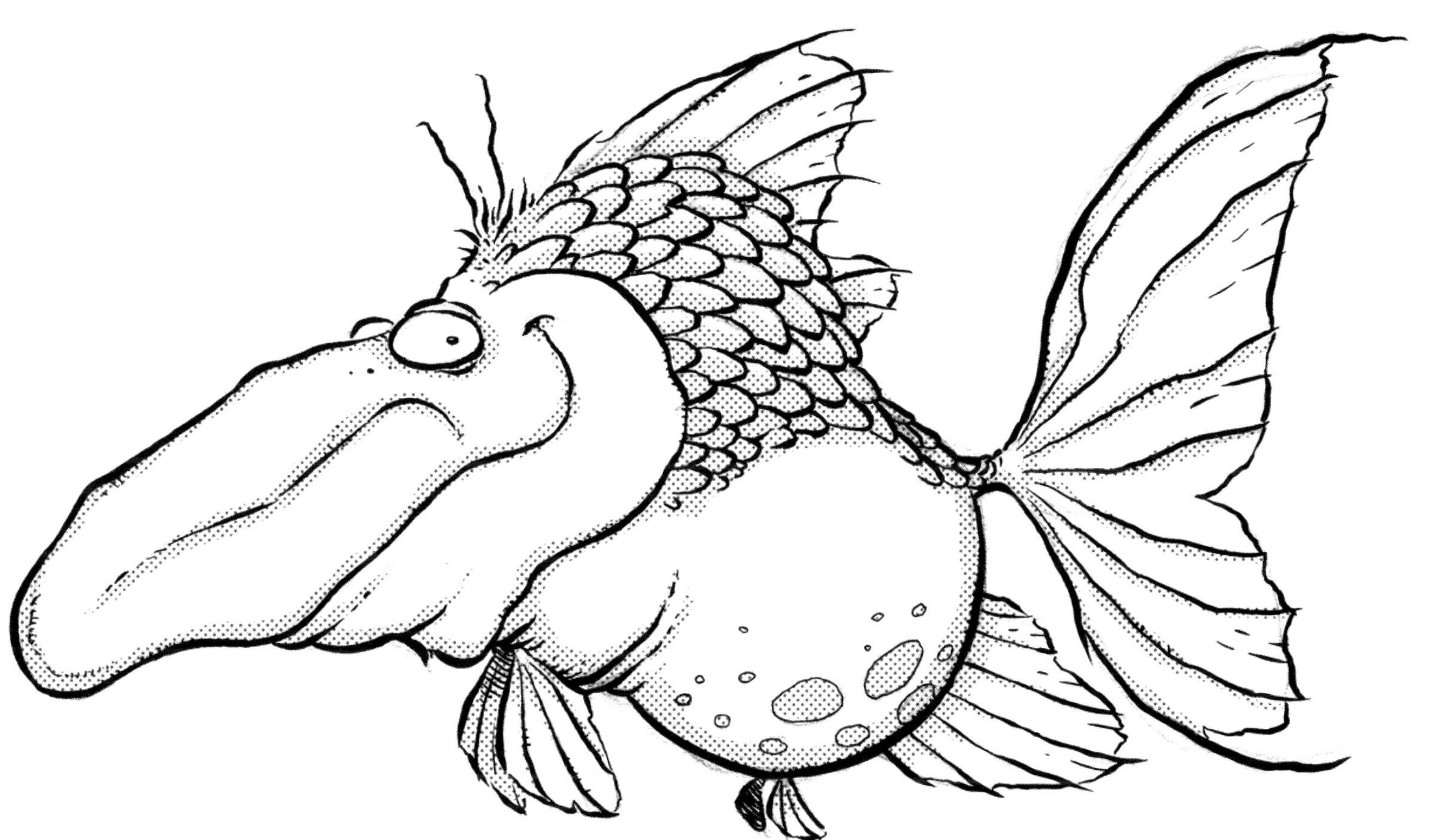

TOP-FLOATING BARNACLE BITER

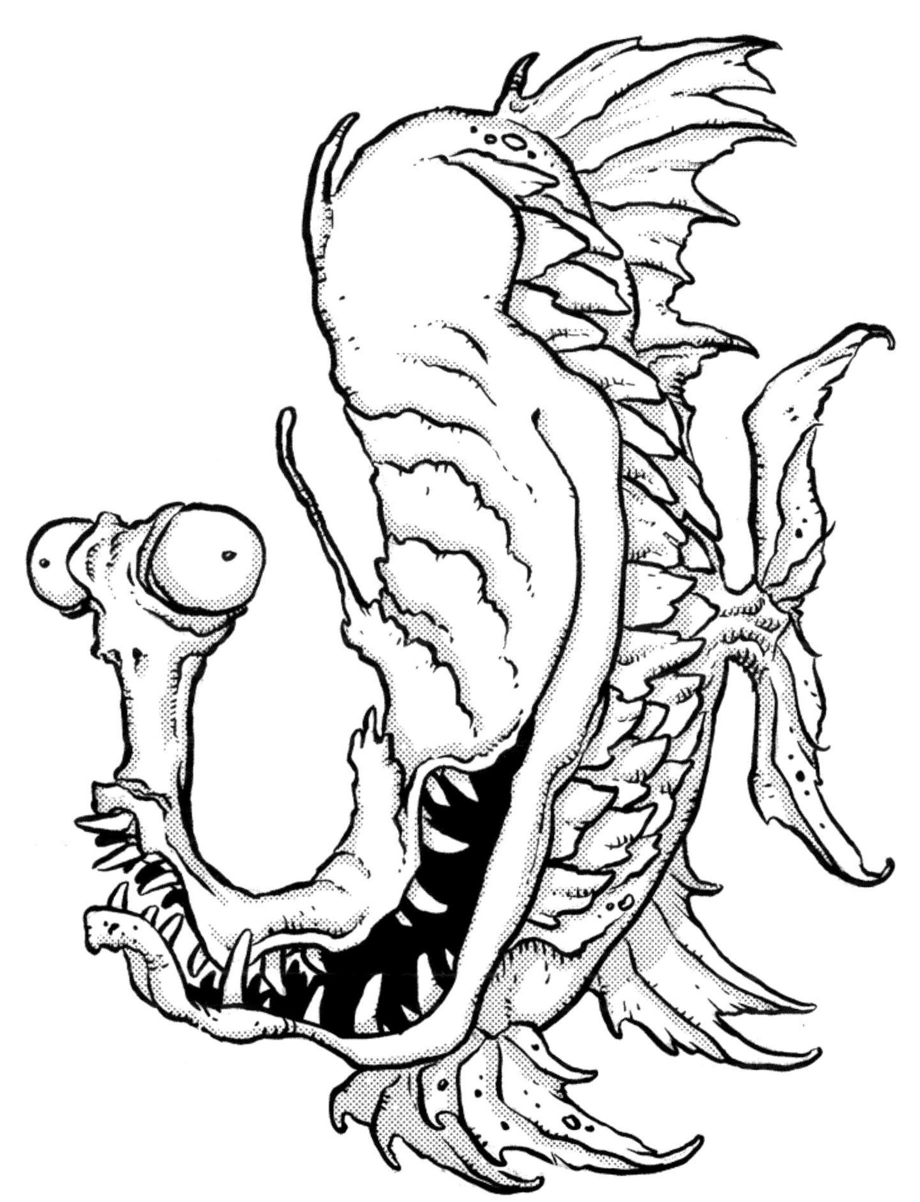

LONG CHIN

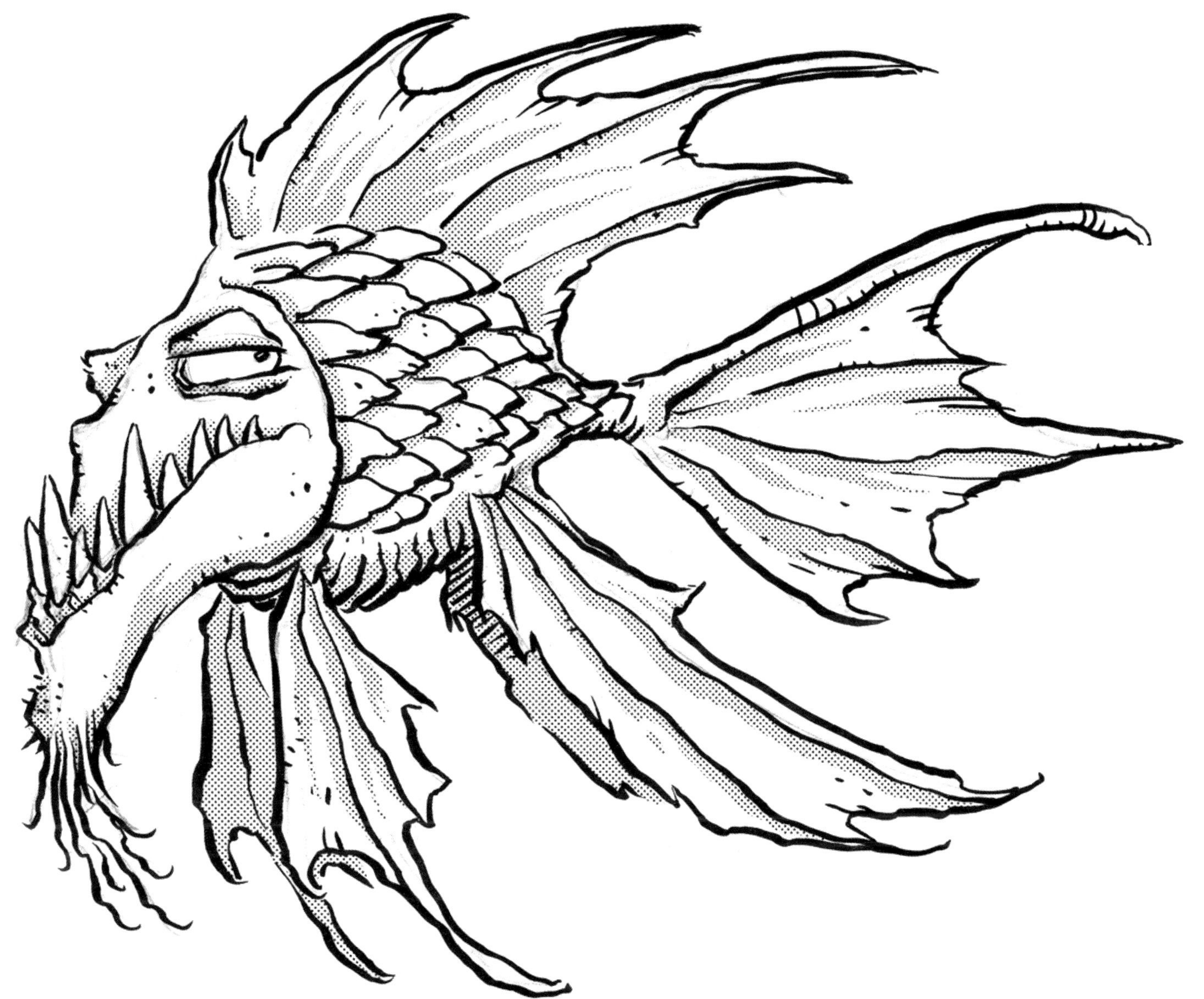

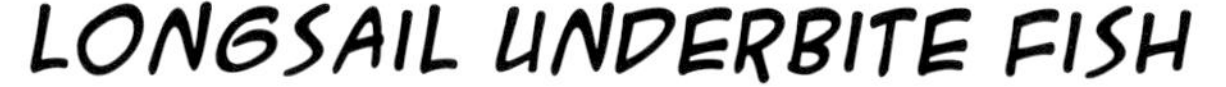
LONGSAIL UNDERBITE FISH

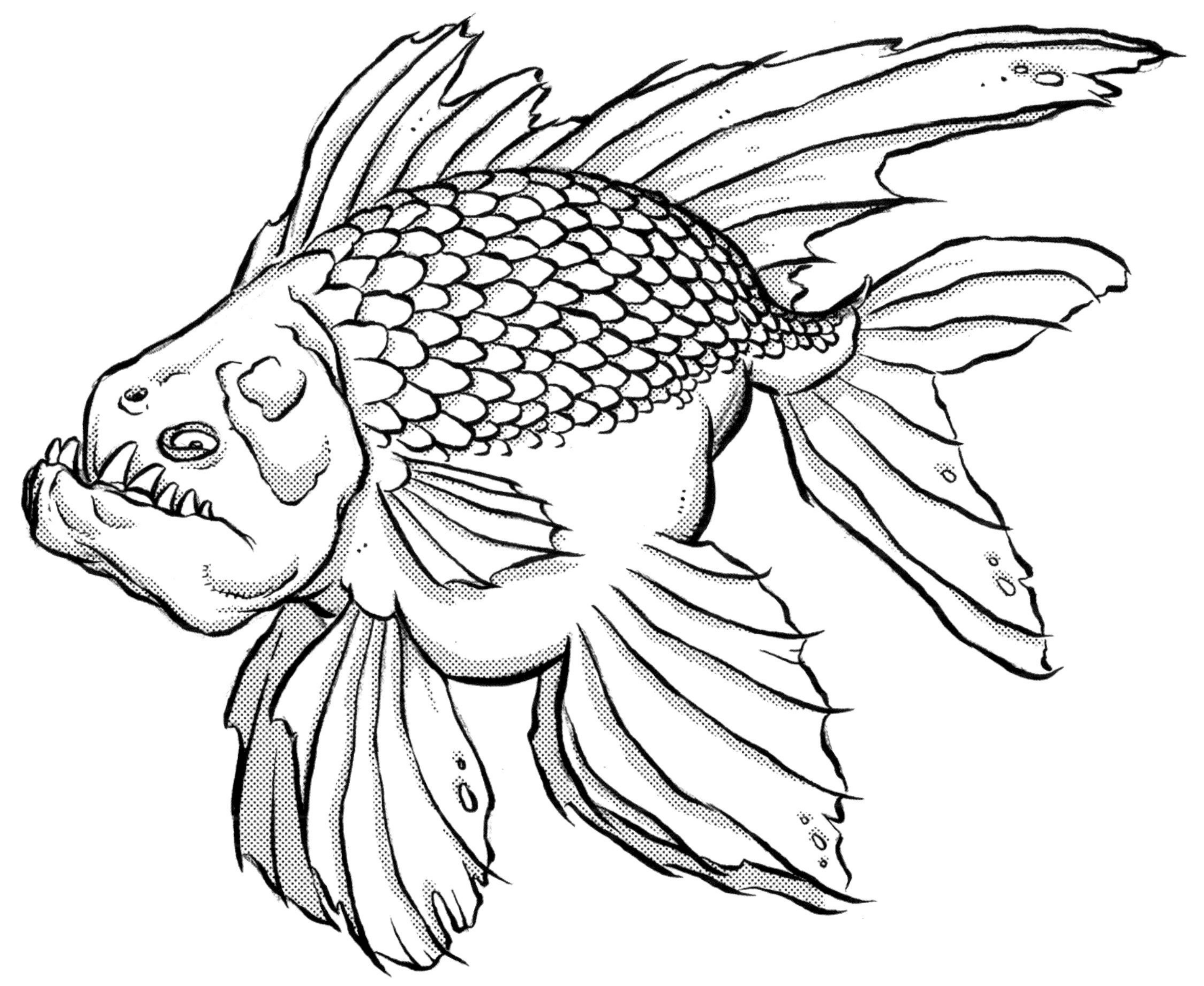

TRUNKFISH

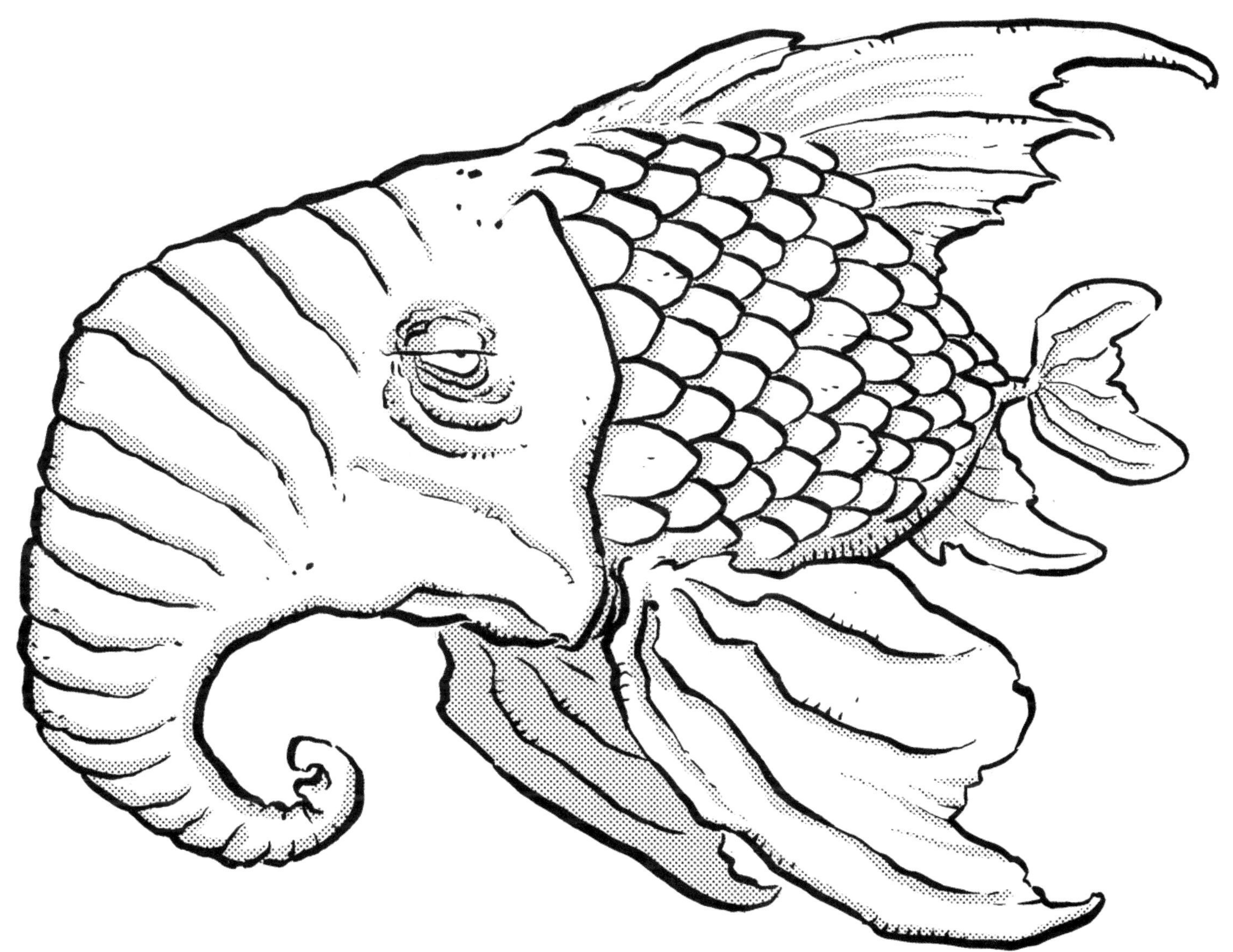

FOO DOG FISH

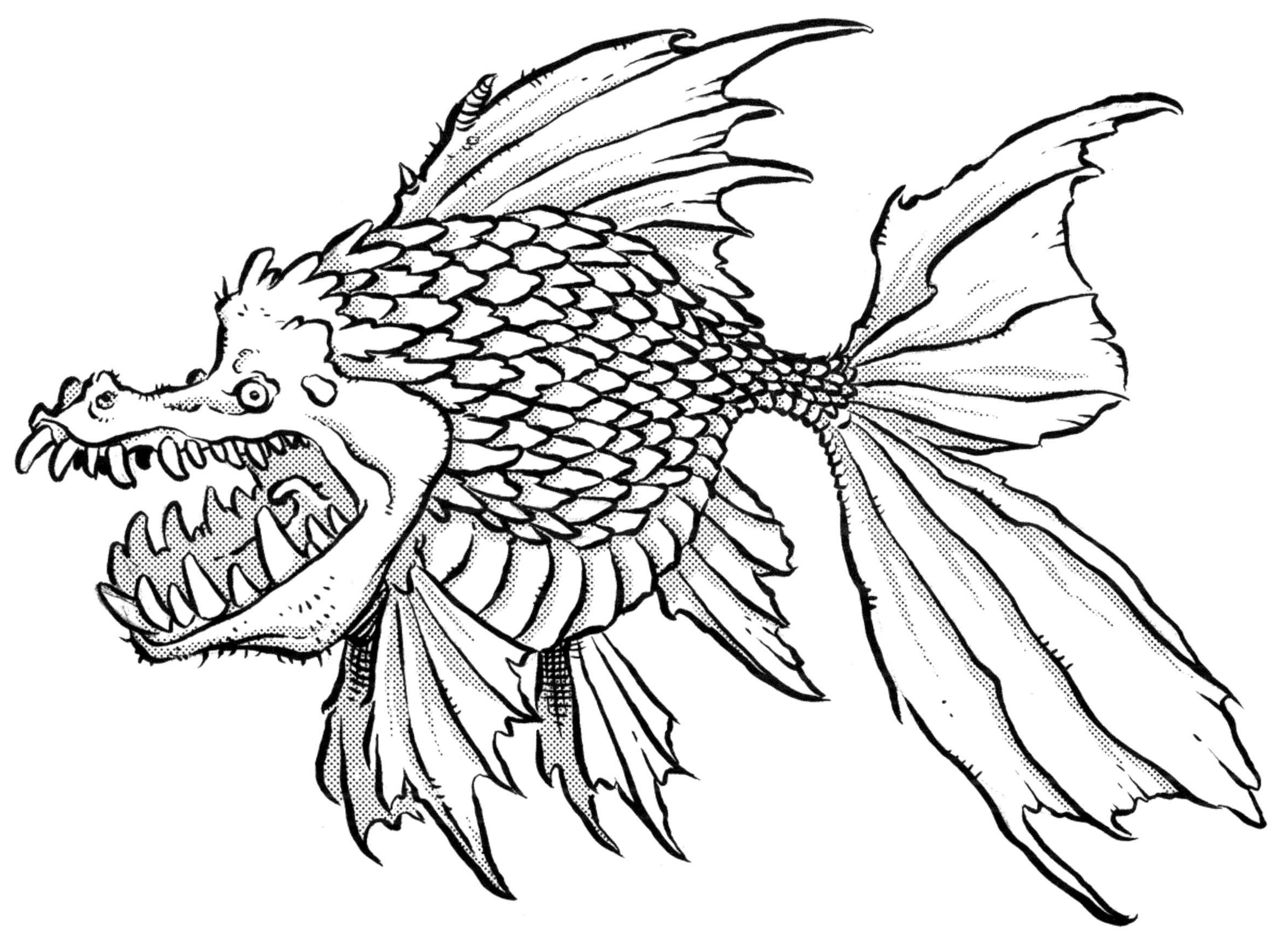

FOREHEAD FISH

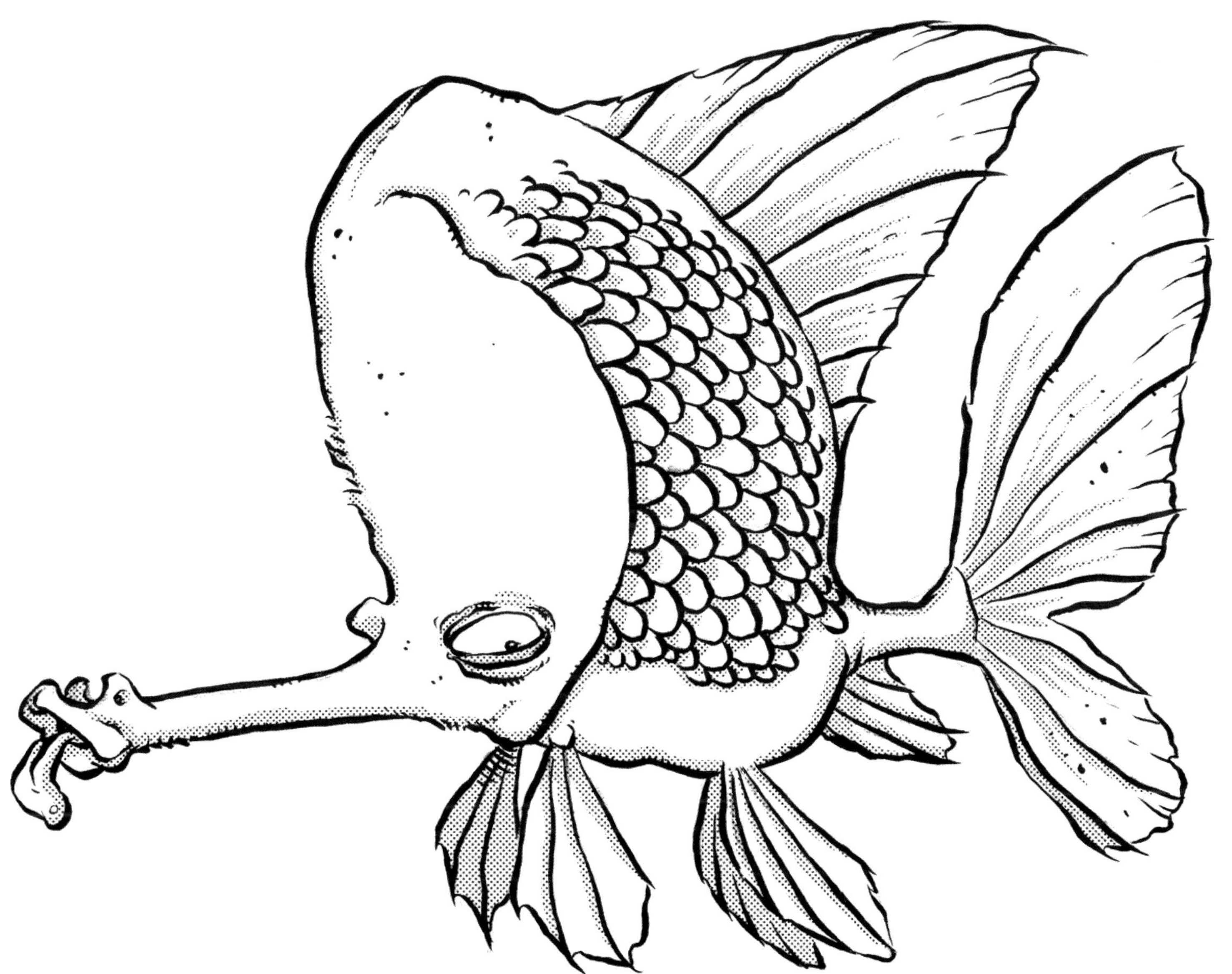

DRAGON KELP EEL

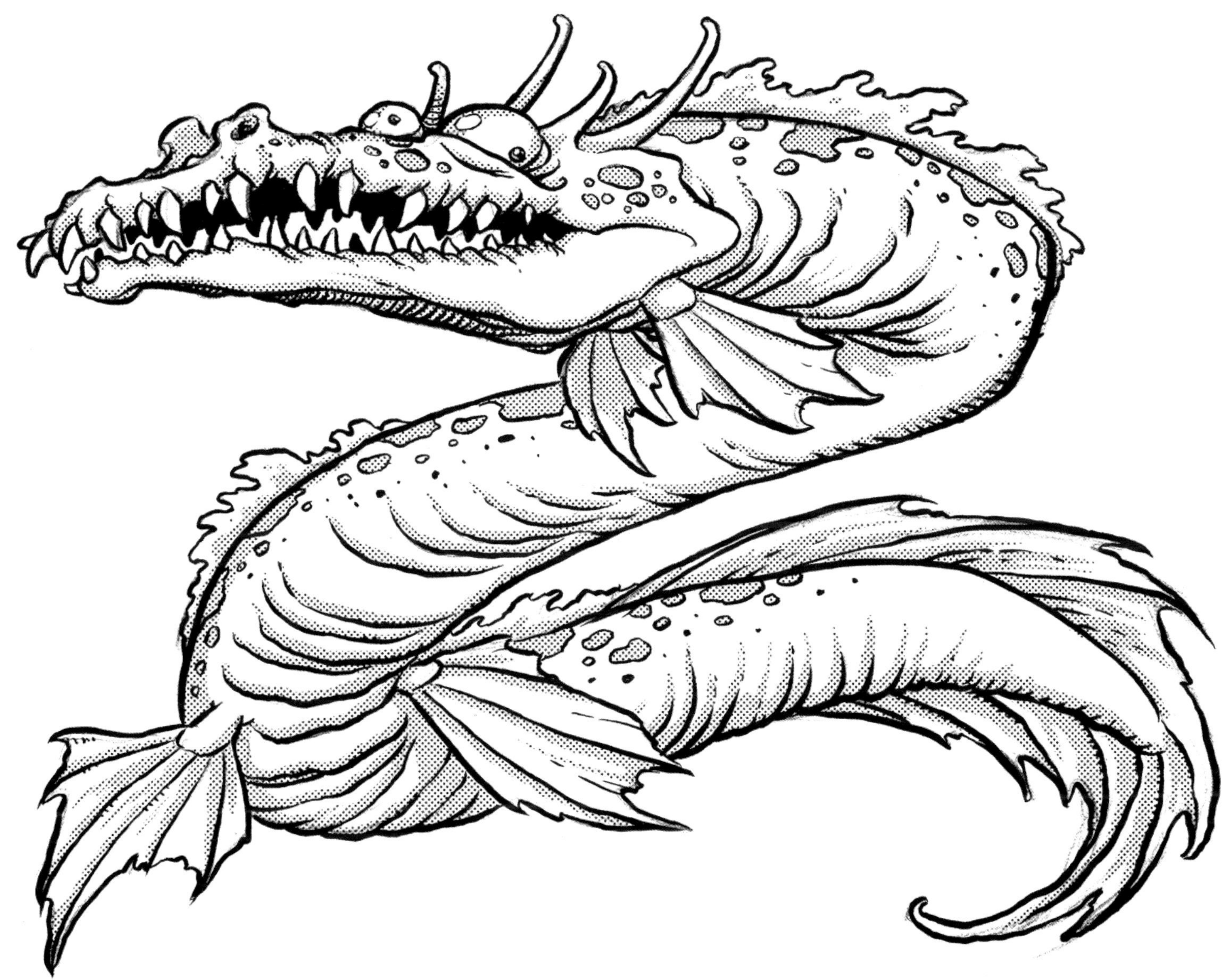

GOOGLY TALLFISH

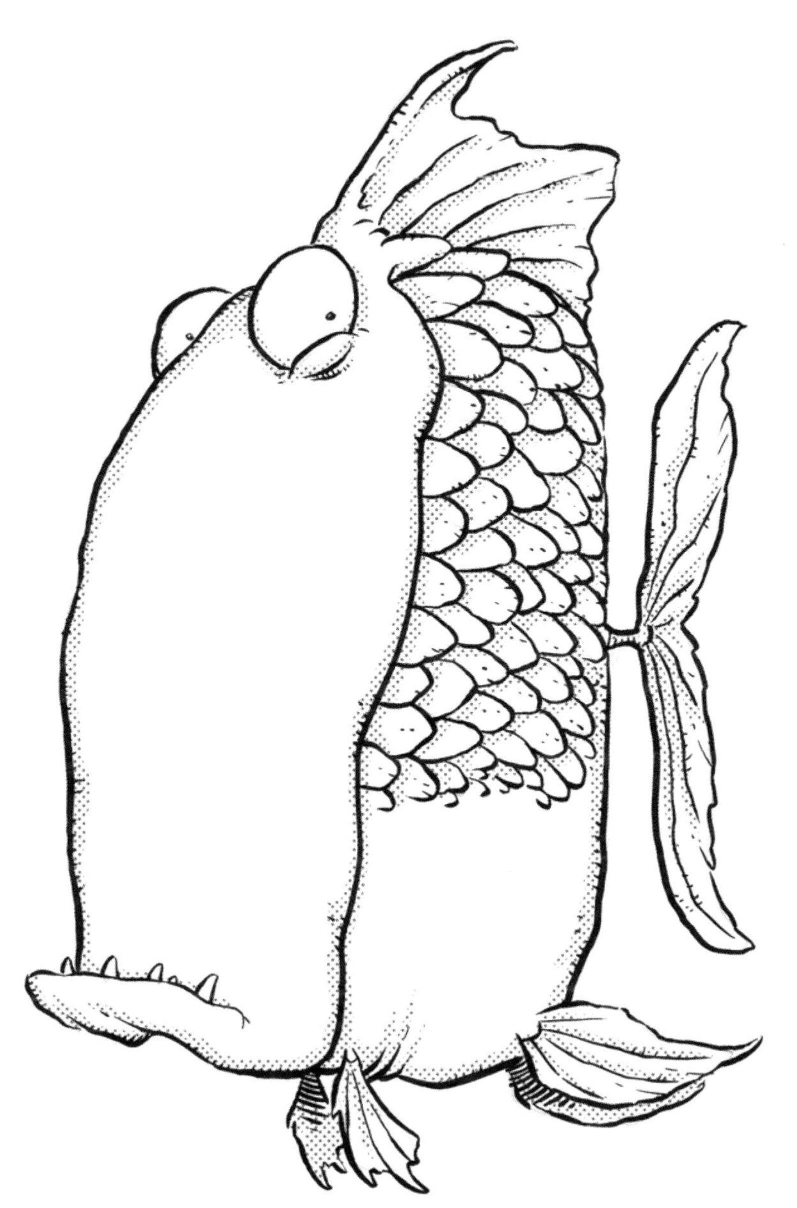

EMMA FISH

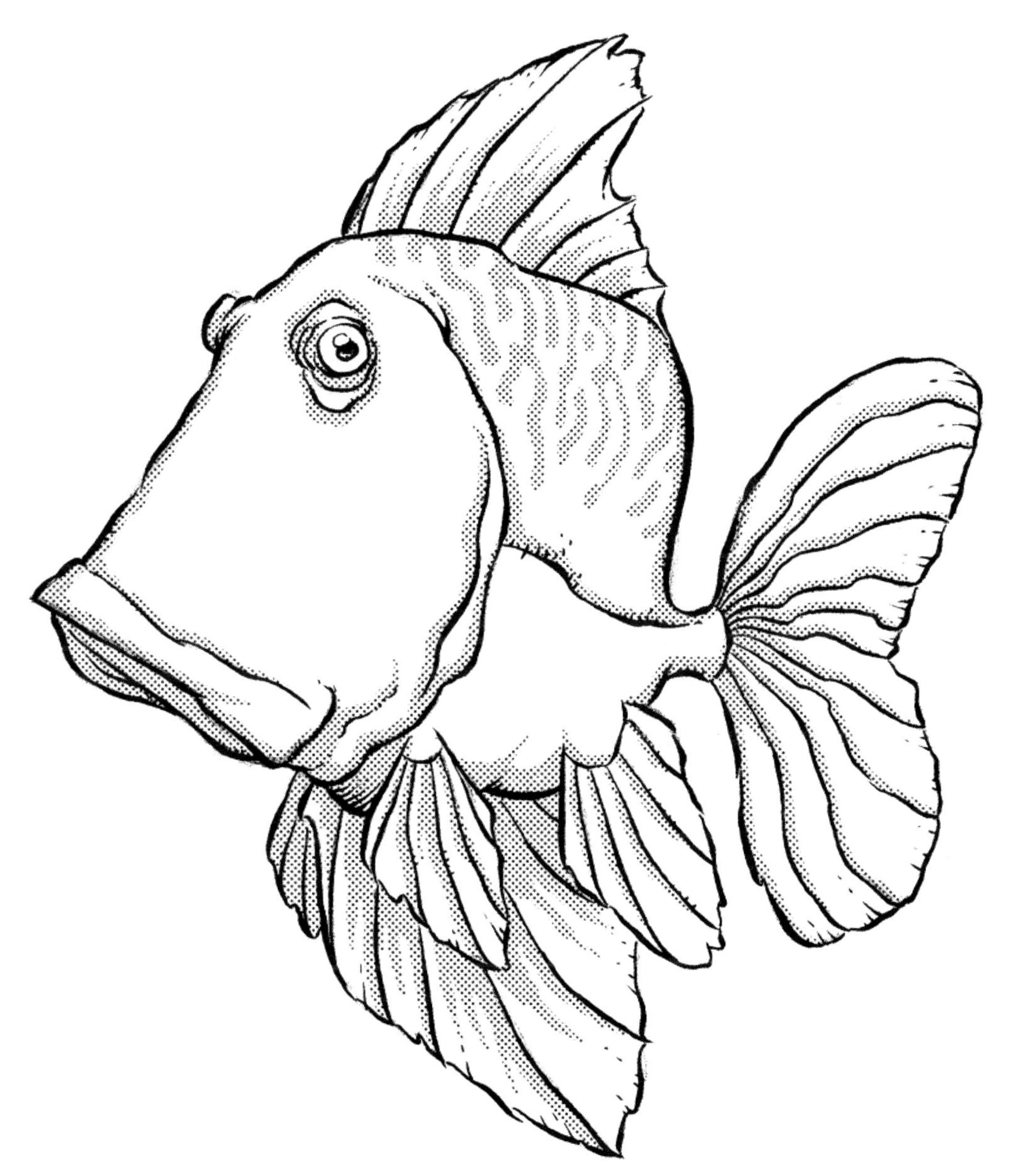

SPOTTED MURK DWELLER

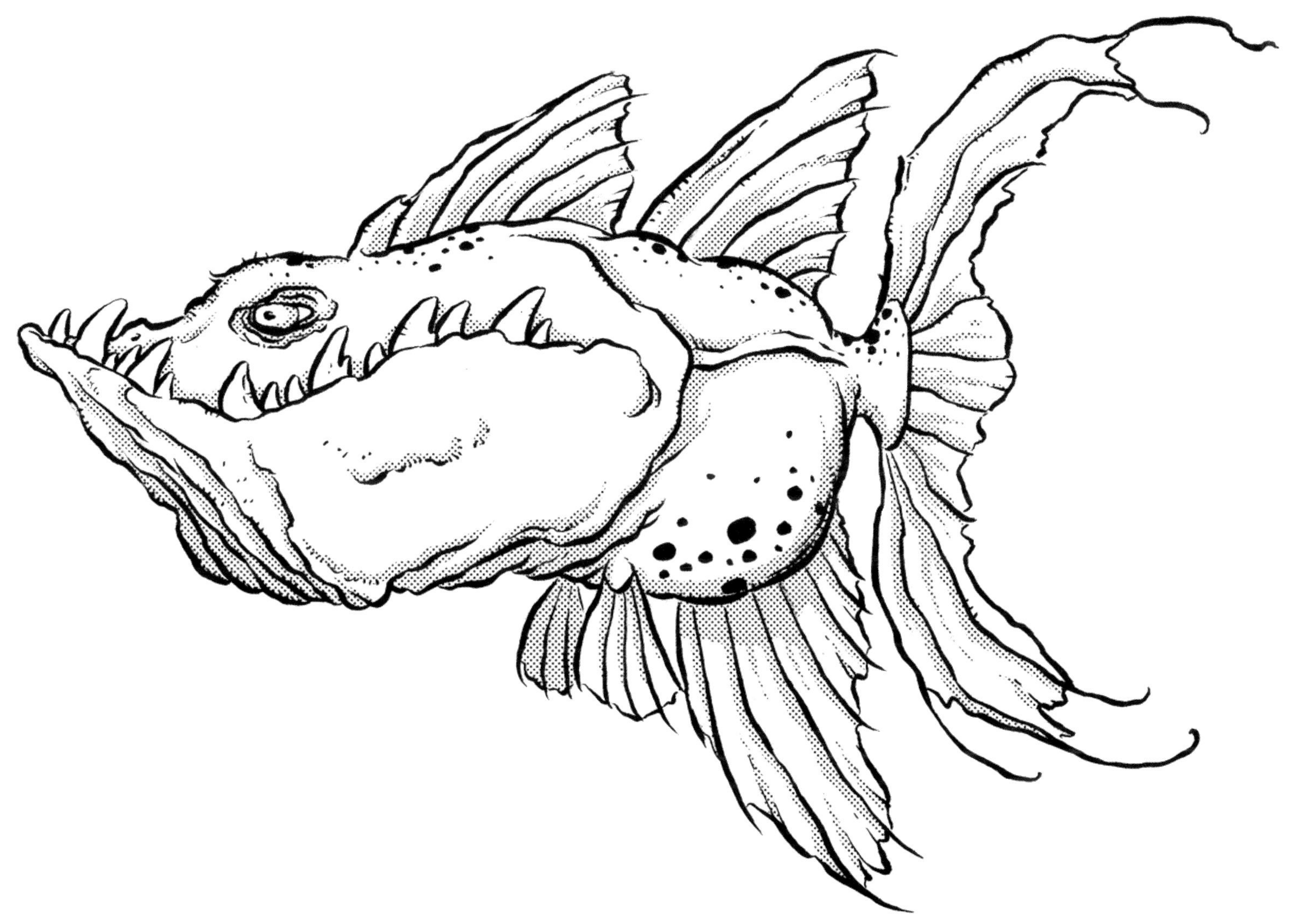

BLUNT NOSE

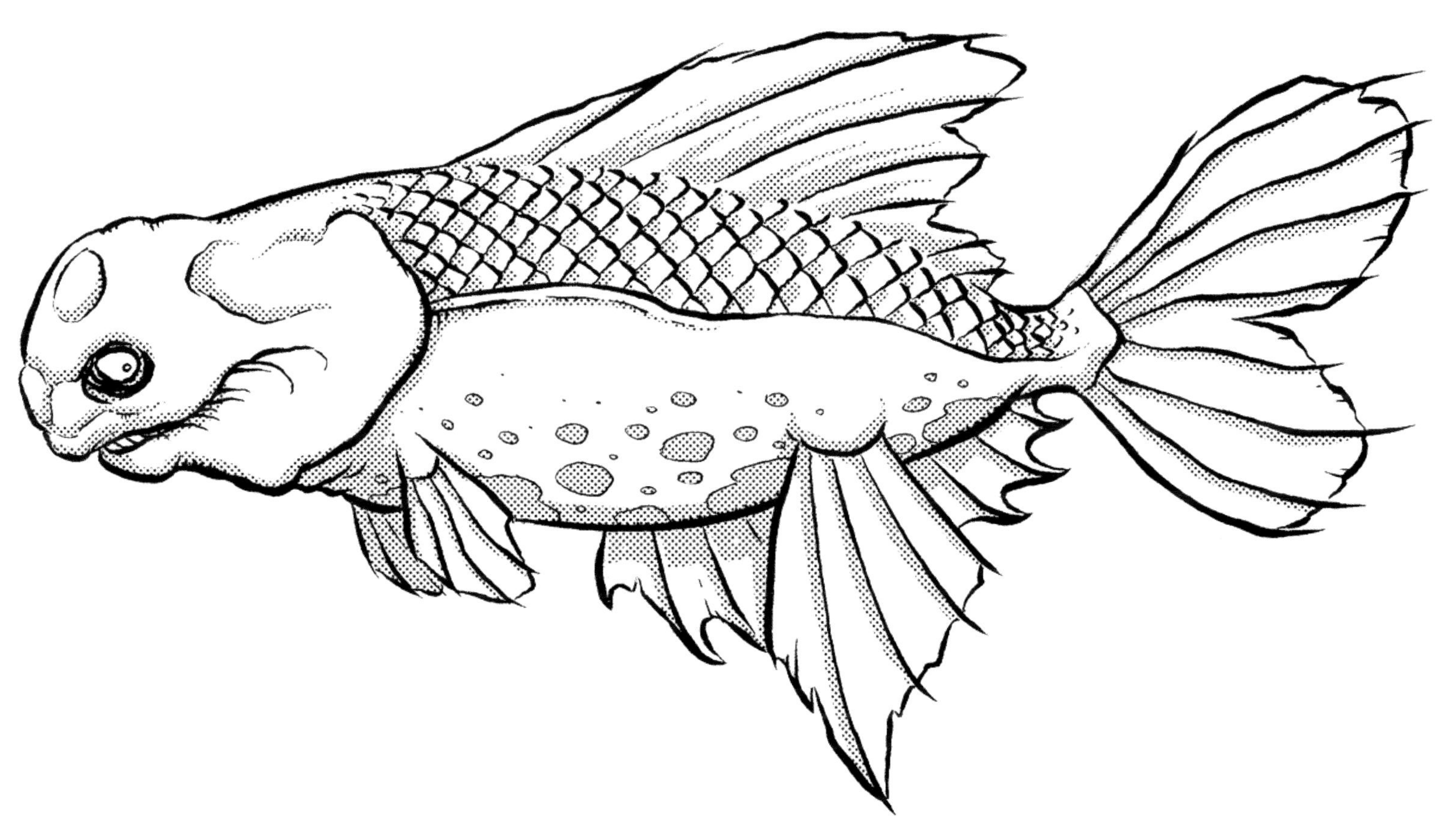

ARMORED LAMPLIGHT FISH

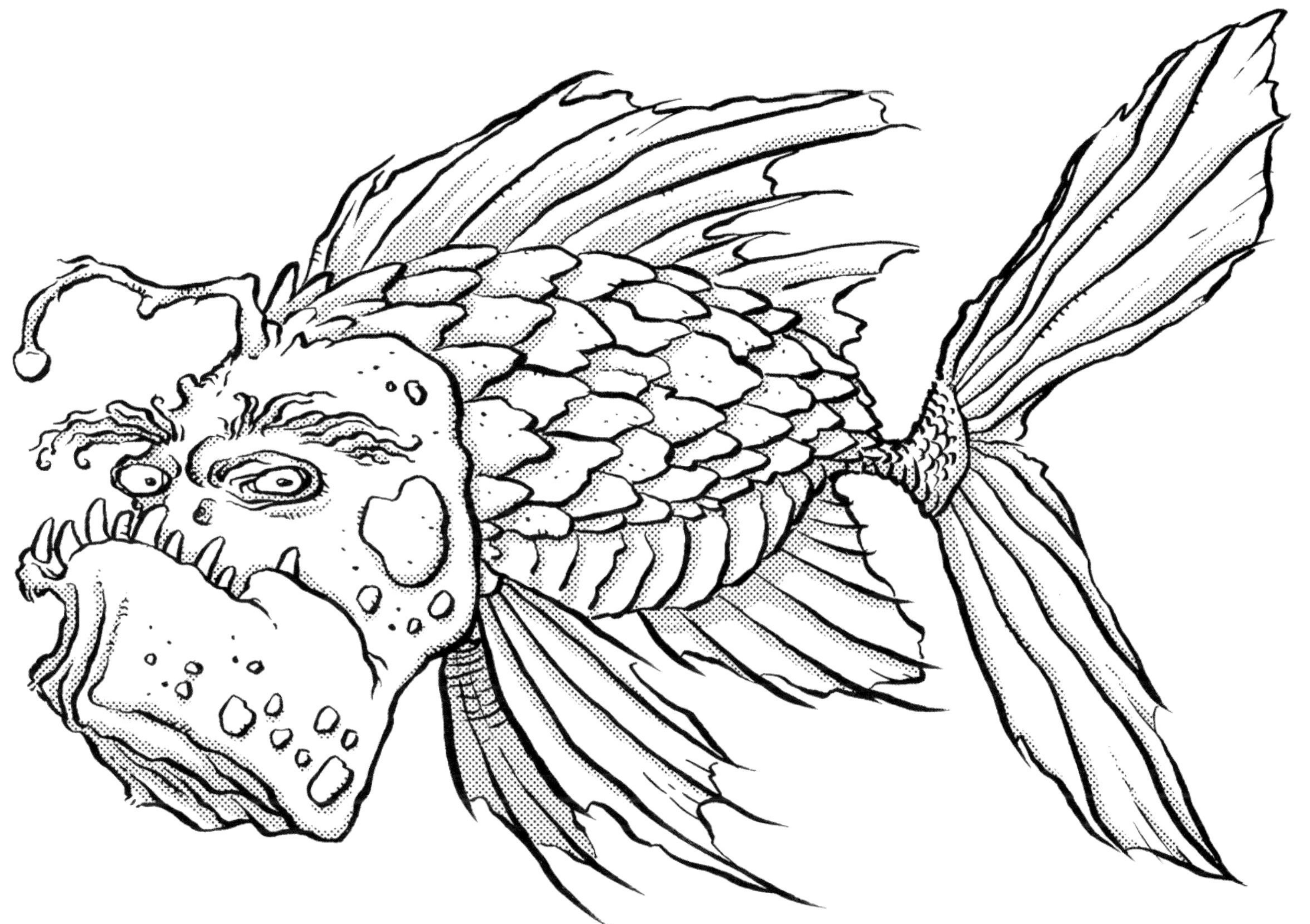

CANYONMOUTH

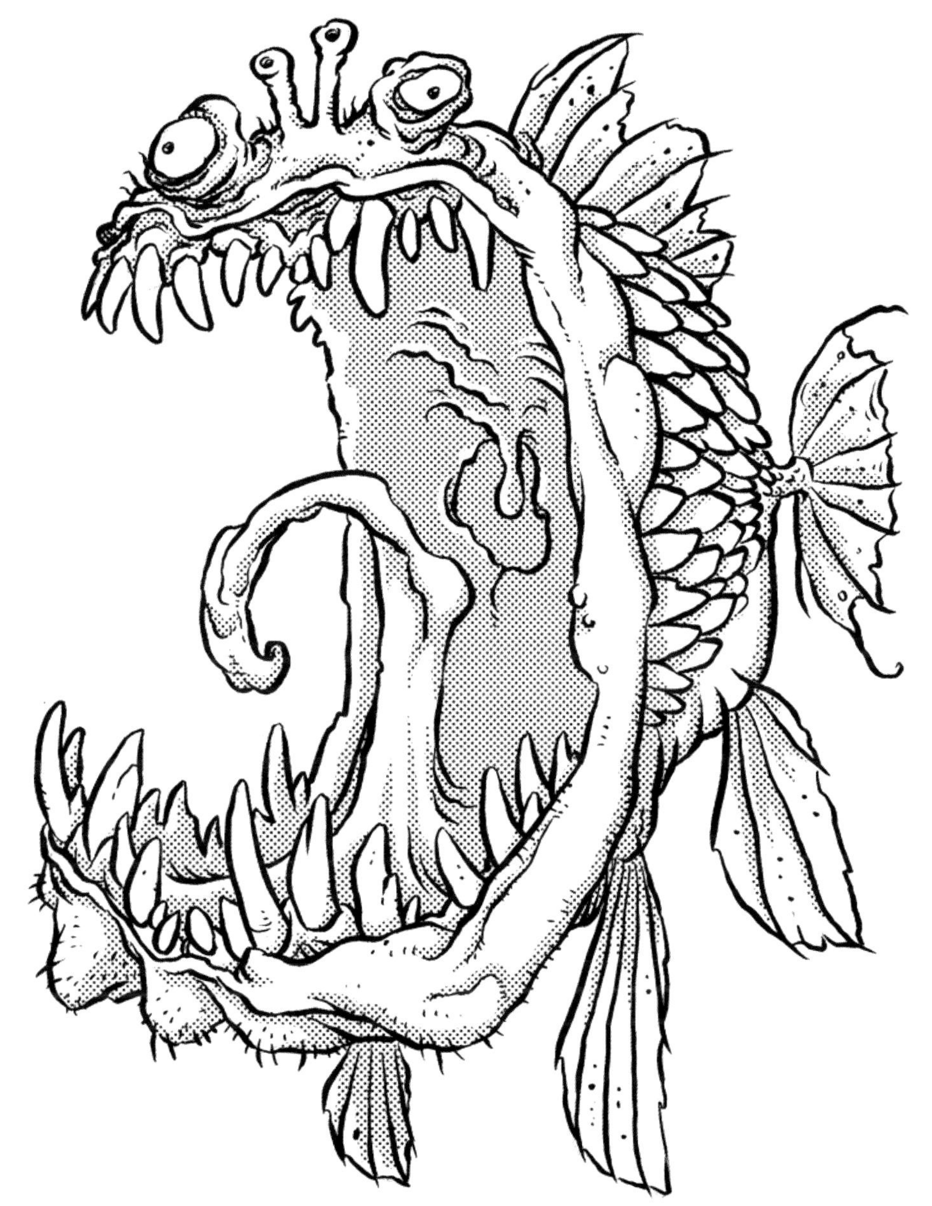

SHAGGY GRUMP

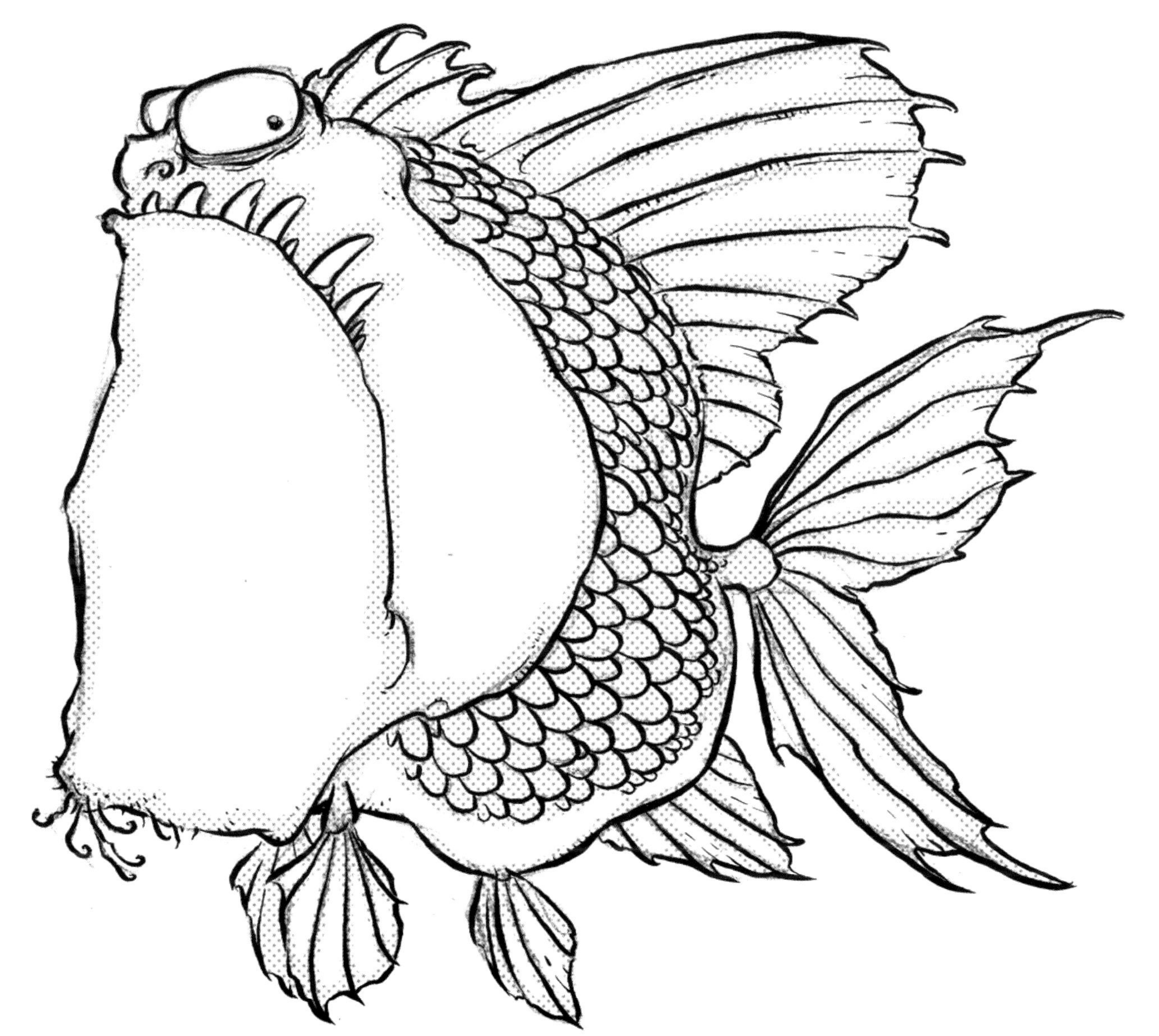

IGNATIUS

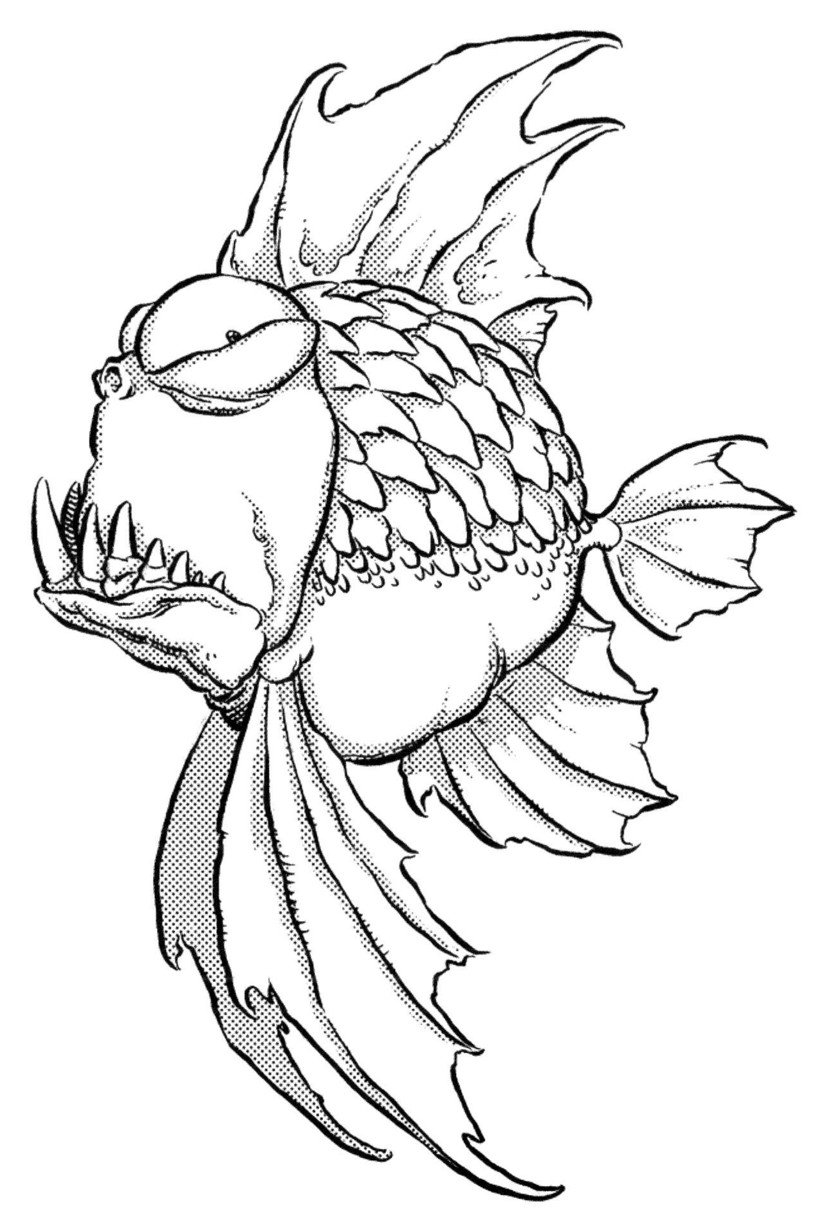

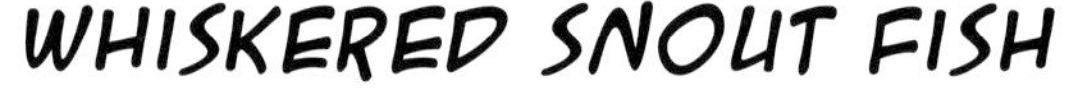
WHISKERED SNOUT FISH

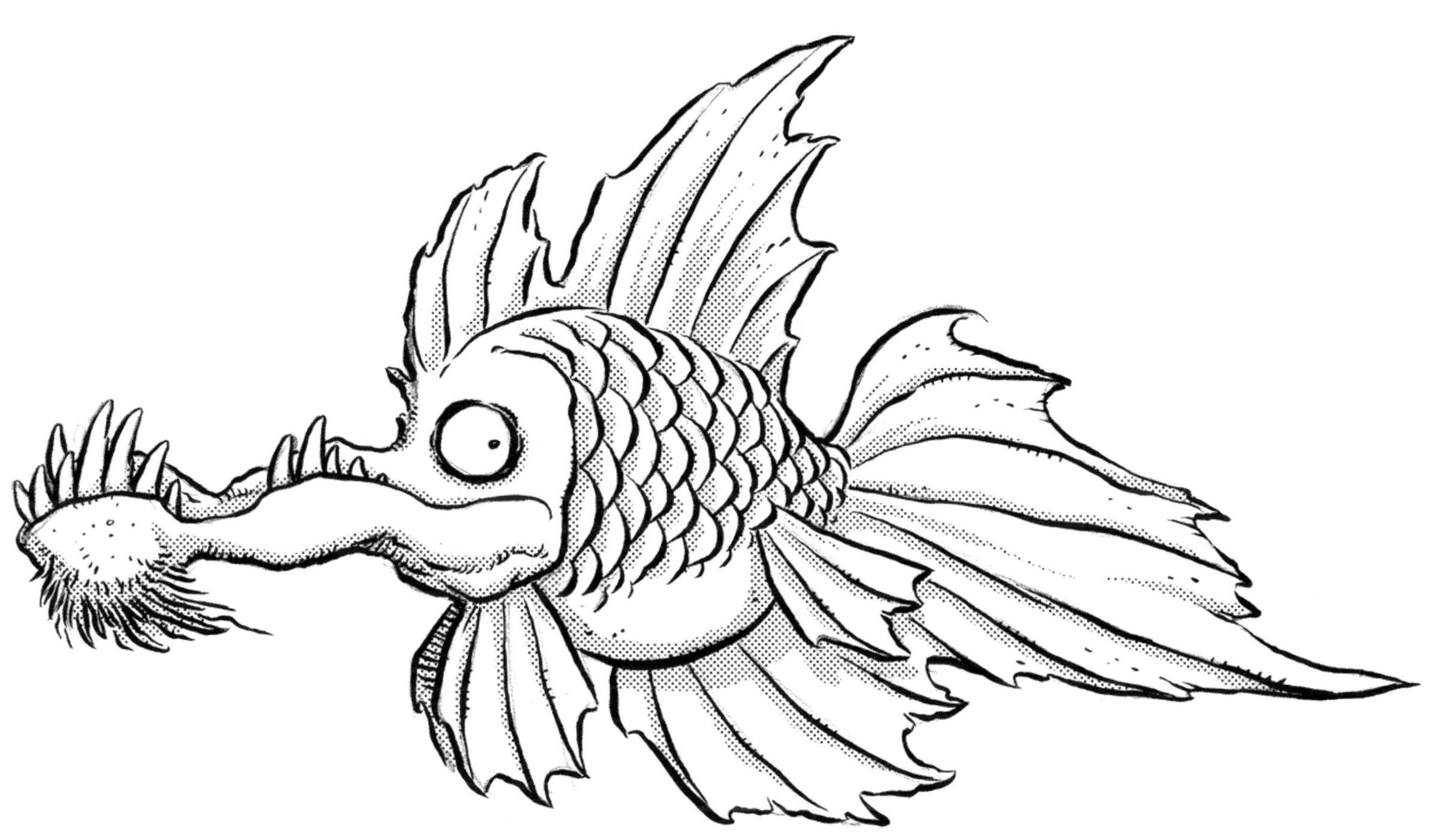

PENSIVE FISH

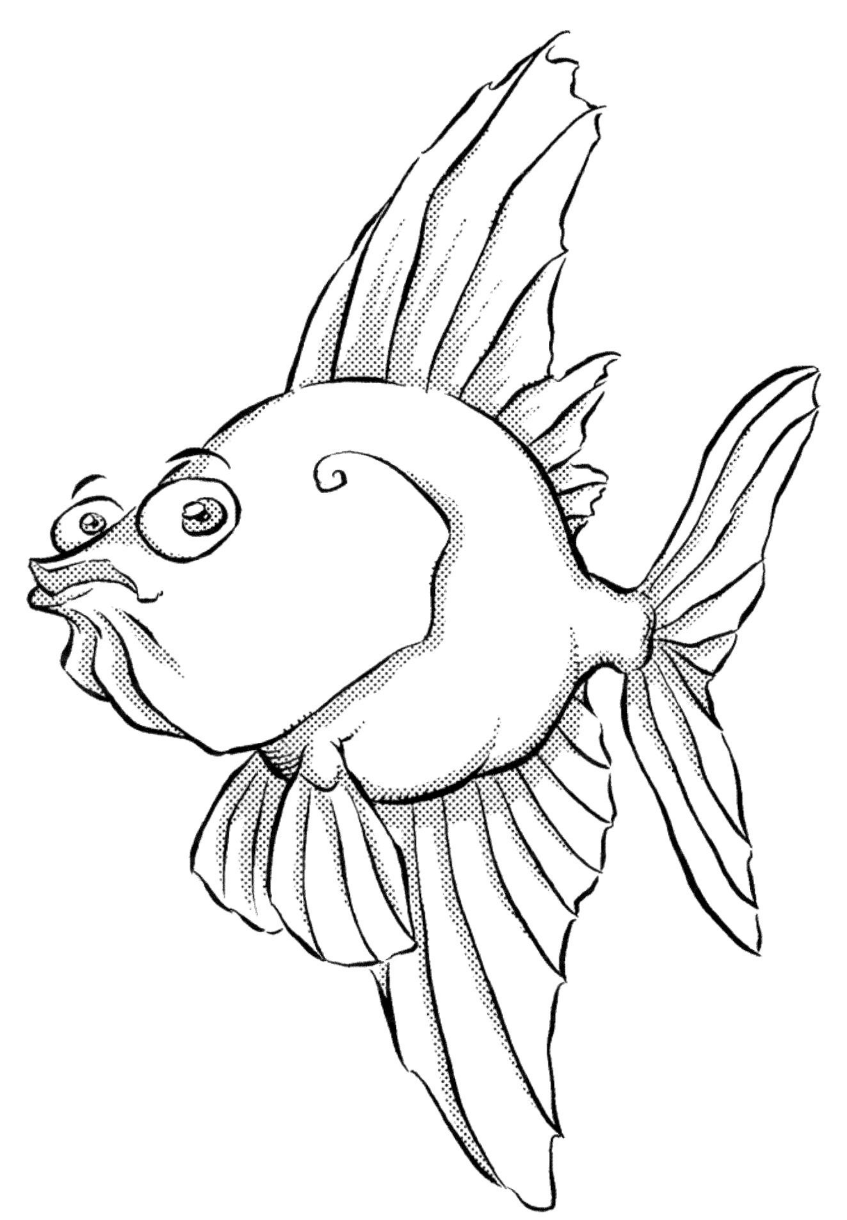

THANK YOU TO JOLENE, AIDEN, AVERY AND CYPRESS.

THANK YOU TO ALL THE KICKSTARTER SUPPORTERS!

STEVE CONLEY, STEVEN "BAT" HILL, DAVE MADDEN, DUSTIN DADE, BRIAN STILLMAN, NAYAN GLUCK, RENEE & MICHAEL ZICKERT, STEVE DUNNE, CHRIS EDRINGTON, RAINE & JEFF HICKMAN, NANCY JO, MARK SENIOR, RUESTER, SEAN CASON, BROOKLYN HENKE, ROY COWING, LAURIE WHEELER, BILL HALLIAR II, JOHN POPSON, RYAN COLLINS, MEECHITY, RICHARD BERES, DYLAN, LARA, ISABEL & JAXON, STEPHANIE THOMPSON, TYLER & SAM, ALANA JOLI FOSTER ABBOTT, HEATHER McNABB, JEFF WAMESTER, NEIL CHRISTOPHER, AMP, JULIA RANGEL, JOSHUA GILLINGHAM, MATT McDONOUGH, GALE MURRIN, JOE & ASHLEY RUSH, THE WINTON FAMILY, JON XAVIER JOHNSON, MARY CLARK, CRYSTAL HERRON, GINGER NINJA, MICHAEL CHAPEL, WOLFBANE-ART, RAY STITH & STACY POGUE-STITH, SCOTT PEZZA, CHRISTOPHER G. WALKER, MARTY MERIDA, ANDREAS KALUZA, GRAHAM BASHFORD, KEVIN C. REAVES, KOUNT VON KULMBACHER, EMILY HARE, HEATHER CURTISS, MARK NASSO, LORI, JENNA & CHRIS GERACI, STEVE PRESCOTT, LEO MEMPHIS & MANUKI, PAUL (PROF), MISSY, CHAZ SUTHERLAND, CAMPBELL ROYALES, FIREWINGS26, PHILL G., ZHE LIU, LOOPYDAVE, SCOTT ZIRKEL, DONNA BURKE, DEAN TANTILLO, TIM DODSON, HUNTER & ZAC GARLAND, RYAN, SHELLEY & MAX MENZE, PAUL BUCKINGHAM, COLTON CARROLL, IVAN KNAPP, L JAMAL WALTON, COLIN SEYMOUR, DANIEL, CONSTANCE HALL, JAMIE M., HOSANNA MOORE, BRICE HOLLIMAN JR., MICHAEL SCHWARTZ, ANDY WELIHOZKIY, SHADOWNET, NATHAN ROSSBERG JAMES, RUTHENIA, MARK A. NELSON, CHET MINTON, BETH MARTIN, BILL PRESSLY, BETH EVES, JOHN MIYASATO, RONAN & FIONA, ZINNIA JOHNDOTTIR, JOHN ZELEZNIK, TOM KENT, ANTHONY DIAZ, JASON FISCHER

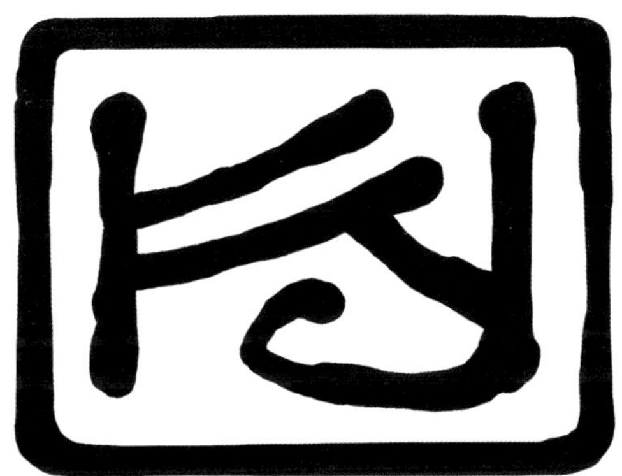

KENNON, WHEN NOT PLAYING BOARD GAMES OR WAITING FOR FOOTBALL SEASON TO START, CAN BE FOUND PAINTING MINIATURES, PLANNING HIS NEXT HIKING TRIP, OR WRITING ABOUT HIMSELF IN THIRD PERSON. HE LIVES IN THE MASSIVE MEGALOPOLIS OF HUTTO, TEXAS WITH WIFE, KIDS, DOG, AND CATS.